IMPACT OF STRESS ON QUALITY OF WORK LIFE AMONG WOMEN EMPLOYEES

B. ZIPPORAH MATILDA

CONTENT

LIST OF TABLES

ABBREVIATIONS

CHAPTER	DESCRIPTION	PAGE NO
I	INTRODUCTION	1 – 20
II	REVIEW OF LITERATURE	21 – 47
III	RESEARCH METHODOLOGY	48 – 52
IV	ANALYSIS AND INTERPRETATION	53 – 127
V	SUMMARY OF FINDINGS, SUGGESTIONS AND CONCLUSION	128 – 144
	BIBLIOGRAPHY	

LIST OF TABLES

TABLE NO	TITLE	PAGE NO
1	TABLE SHOWING PERSONAL CHARACTERISTICS	54
2	TABLE SHOWING EMPLOYMENT CHARACTERISTICS	56
3	TABLE SHOWING EXPLORATORY FACTOR ANALYSIS – ORGANISATIONAL CAUSES OF STRESS	58
4	TABLE SHOWING DESCRIPTIVE STATISTICS	61
5	TABLE SHOWING TEST OF NORMALITY	62
6	TABLE SHOWING CLUSTER AND DISCRIMINANT ANALYSIS - ORGANISATIONAL CAUSES OF STRESS GROUPS	63
7	TABLE SHOWING MEAN DIFFERENCES BETWEEN AREA OF LIVING AND ORGANISATIONAL CAUSES OF STRESS – TOTAL SCORE & ITS FACTORS	65
8	TABLE SHOWING MEAN DIFFERENCES BETWEEN NATURE OF THE FAMILY AND ORGANISATIONAL CAUSES OF STRESS – TOTAL SCORE & ITS FACTORS	66
9	TABLE SHOWING MEAN DIFFERENCES BETWEEN MARITAL STATUS AND ORGANISATIONAL CAUSES OF STRESS – TOTAL SCORE & ITS FACTORS	67
10	TABLE SHOWING MEAN DIFFERENCES BETWEEN NATURE OF THE ORGANISATION AND ORGANISATIONAL CAUSES OF STRESS – TOTAL SCORE & ITS FACTORS	68
11	TABLE SHOWING MEAN DIFFERENCES BETWEEN AGE AND ORGANISATIONAL CAUSES OF STRESS – TOTAL SCORE & ITS FACTORS	69
12	TABLE SHOWING MEAN DIFFERENCES BETWEEN EDUCATIONAL QUALIFICATION AND ORGANISATIONAL CAUSES OF STRESS – TOTAL SCORE & ITS FACTORS	70

TABLE NO	TITLE	PAGE NO
13	TABLE SHOWING DIFFERENCES BETWEEN INCOME AND ORGANISATIONAL CAUSES OF STRESS – TOTAL SCORE & ITS FACTORS	71
14	TABLE SHOWING MEAN DIFFERENCES BETWEEN JOB NATURE AND ORGANISATIONAL CAUSES OF STRESS – TOTAL SCORE & ITS FACTORS	72
15	TABLE SHOWING DIFFERENCES BETWEEN LEVEL OF EMPLOYMENT AND ORGANISATIONAL CAUSES OF STRESS – TOTAL SCORE & ITS FACTORS	73
16	TABLE SHOWING EXPLORATORY FACTOR ANALYSIS – PERSONAL CAUSES OF STRESS	75
17	TABLE SHOWING DESCRIPTIVE STATISTICS – PERSONAL CAUSES OF STRESS	77
18	TABLE SHOWING TEST OF NORMALITY – PERSONAL CAUSES OF STRESS	78
19	TABLE SHOWING CLUSTER AND DISCRIMINANT ANALYSIS - PERSONAL CAUSES OF STRESS GROUPS	79
20	TABLE SHOWING DIFFERENCES BETWEEN AREA OF LIVING AND PERSONAL CAUSES OF STRESS – TOTAL SCORE & ITS FACTORS	81
21	TABLE SHOWING DIFFERENCES BETWEEN NATURE OF THE FAMILY AND PERSONAL CAUSES OF STRESS – TOTAL SCORE & ITS FACTORS	82
22	TABLE SHOWING DIFFERENCES BETWEEN MARITAL STATUS AND PERSONAL CAUSES OF STRESS – TOTAL SCORE & ITS FACTORS	83
23	TABLE SHOWING DIFFERENCES BETWEEN NATURE OF THE ORGANISATION AND PERSONAL CAUSES OF STRESS – TOTAL SCORE & ITS FACTORS	84

TABLE NO	TITLE	PAGE NO
24	TABLE SHOWING DIFFERENCES BETWEEN AGE AND PERSONAL CAUSES OF STRESS – TOTAL SCORE & ITS FACTORS	85
25	TABLE SHOWING DIFFERENCES BETWEEN EDUCATIONAL QUALIFICATION AND PERSONAL CAUSES OF STRESS – TOTAL SCORE & ITS FACTORS	86
26	TABLE SHOWING DIFFERENCES BETWEEN INCOME AND PERSONAL CAUSES OF STRESS – TOTAL SCORE & ITS FACTORS	87
27	TABLE SHOWING DIFFERENCES BETWEEN JOB NATURE AND PERSONAL CAUSES OF STRESS – TOTAL SCORE & ITS FACTORS	88
28	TABLE SHOWING DIFFERENCES BETWEEN LEVEL OF EMPLOYMENT AND PERSONAL CAUSES OF STRESS – TOTAL SCORE & ITS FACTORS	89
29	IMPORTANCE REDUCE STRESS TABLE SHOWING EXPLORATORY FACTOR ANALYSIS – IMPORTANCE REDUCE STRESS	91
30	TABLE SHOWING DESCRIPTIVE STATISTICS	93
31	TABLE SHOWING TEST OF NORMALITY	94
32	TABLE SHOWING CLUSTER AND DISCRIMINANT ANALYSIS – IMPORTANCE TO REDUCE STRESS GROUPS	95
33	TABLE SHOWING DIFFERENCES BETWEEN AREA OF LIVING AND IMPORTANCE REDUCE STRESS – TOTAL SCORE & ITS FACTORS	97
34	TABLE SHOWING DIFFERENCES BETWEEN NATURE OF THE FAMILY AND IMPORTANCE REDUCE STRESS – TOTAL SCORE & ITS FACTORS	98

TABLE NO	TITLE	PAGE NO
35	TABLE SHOWING DIFFERENCES BETWEEN MARITAL STATUS AND IMPORTANCE REDUCE STRESS – TOTAL SCORE & ITS FACTORS	99
36	TABLE SHOWING DIFFERENCES BETWEEN NATURE OF THE ORGANISATION AND IMPORTANCE REDUCE STRESS – TOTAL SCORE & ITS FACTORS	100
37	TABLE SHOWING DIFFERENCES BETWEEN AGE AND IMPORTANCE REDUCE STRESS – TOTAL SCORE & ITS FACTORS	101
38	TABLE SHOWING DIFFERENCES BETWEEN EDUCATIONAL QUALIFICATION AND IMPORTANCE REDUCE STRESS – TOTAL SCORE & ITS FACTORS	102
39	TABLE SHOWING DIFFERENCES BETWEEN INCOME AND IMPORTANCE REDUCE STRESS – TOTAL SCORE & ITS FACTORS	103
40	TABLE SHOWING DIFFERENCES BETWEEN JOB NATURE AND IMPORTANCE REDUCE STRESS – TOTAL SCORE & ITS FACTORS	104
41	TABLE SHOWING DIFFERENCES BETWEEN LEVEL OF EMPLOYMENT AND IMPORTANCE REDUCE STRESS – TOTAL SCORE & ITS FACTORS	105
42	TABLE SHOWING EXPLORATORY FACTOR ANALYSIS – QUALITY OF WORK LIFE	107
43	TABLE SHOWING DESCRIPTIVE STATISTICS	109
44	TABLE SHOWING TEST OF NORMALITY	110
45	TABLE SHOWING CLUSTER AND DISCRIMINANT ANALYSIS - QUALITY WORK LIFE GROUPS	111
46	TABLE SHOWING DIFFERENCES BETWEEN AREA OF LIVING AND QUALITY WORK LIFE – TOTAL SCORE & ITS FACTORS	113

TABLE NO	TITLE	PAGE NO
47	TABLE SHOWING DIFFERENCES BETWEEN NATURE OF THE FAMILY AND QUALITY WORK LIFE – TOTAL SCORE & ITS FACTORS	114
48	TABLE SHOWING DIFFERENCES BETWEEN MARITAL STATUS AND QUALITY WORK LIFE – TOTAL SCORE & ITS FACTORS	115
49	TABLE SHOWING DIFFERENCES BETWEEN NATURE OF THE ORGANISATION AND QUALITY WORK LIFE – TOTAL SCORE & ITS FACTORS	116
50	TABLE SHOWING DIFFERENCES BETWEEN AGE AND QUALITY WORK LIFE – TOTAL SCORE & ITS FACTORS	117
51	TABLE SHOWING DIFFERENCES BETWEEN EDUCATIONAL QUALIFICATION AND QUALITY WORK LIFE – TOTAL SCORE & ITS FACTORS	118
52	TABLE SHOWING DIFFERENCES BETWEEN INCOME AND QUALITY WORK LIFE – TOTAL SCORE & ITS FACTORS	119
53	TABLE SHOWING DIFFERENCES BETWEEN JOB NATURE AND QUALITY WORK LIFE – TOTAL SCORE & ITS FACTORS	120
54	TABLE SHOWING DIFFERENCES BETWEEN LEVEL OF EMPLOYMENT AND QUALITY WORK LIFE – TOTAL SCORE & ITS FACTORS	121
55	TABLE SHOWING STRUCTURAL EQUATION MODELING – DETERMINANTS OF QUALITY OF WORK LIFE	123
56	TABLE SHOWING CRITERIA FOR STRUCTURAL EQUATION MODEL ANALYSIS	125
57	SIGNIFICANT PREDICTOR OF QUALITY OF WORK LIFE	126

ABBREVIATIONS

CVD	CARDIOVASCULAR DISEASE
DCM	DEMAND CONTROL MODEL
OCS	ORGANISATIONAL CAUSES OF STRESS
PCS	PERSONAL CAUSES OF STRESS
FRMRS	FULFILLMENT OF REMEDICAL MEASURE TO REDUCES OF STRESS
QWL	QUALITY OF WORK LIFE
OCF	ORGANISATIONAL CLIMATE FACTOR
MAF	MANAGERIAL ASPECTS FACTOR
MCPARS	MANAGEMENT COMPETENCIES FOR PREVENTING AND REDUCING STRESS
WHO	WORLD HEALTH ORGANIZATION
ILO	INTERNATIONAL LABOUR ORGANIZATION
EI	EMOTIONAL INTELLIGENCE
P-O	PERSON-ORGANIZATION
C-PMs,	CASE PROCESSING AND MANAGEMENT SYSTEM.
AMOS	ANALYSIS OF A MOMENT STRUCTURES

DGM	DEPUTY GENERAL MANAGER
ORS	ORGANIZATIONAL ROLE STRESS
GFI	GOODNESS OF FIT INDEX
AGFI	ADJUSTED GOODNESS OF FIT INDEX
CFI	COMPARATIVE FIT INDEX
RMR	ROOT MEAN SQUARE RESIDUALS
RMSEA	ROOT MEAN SQUARE ERROR OF APPROXIMATION
SEM	STRUCTURAL EQUATION MODELING
KMO	KAISER-MEYER-OLKIN
BTS	BARTLETT'S TEST OF SPHERICITY
JEF	JOB ENRICHMENT FACTOR
JENF	JOB ENLARGEMENT FACTOR
IRS	IMPORTANCE TO REDUCE STRESS
JDF	JOB DESCRIPTION FACTOR
JSF	JOB STRUCTURE FACTOR
WLBF	WORK LIFE IMBALANCE FACTOR
WHF	WORK HINDRANCE FACTOR

Chapter I

INTRODUCTION

CHAPTER – I
INTRODUCTION

1.1 INTRODUCTION

Gone are the days when ladies were meant only for the household works. The present period witness the changing mentality of the women towards their own transformation from being a typical housewife to being a successful business woman. Parents are encouraging their children equally. In this challenging scenario, stress plays an important role in their life. We are able to observe the various facets that are hidden within a woman. Men also support women to excel in their fields by providing the needed help in the house hold activities. Also, the society as a whole has understood the capability of woman and provides various alternatives for woman to come out and explore the business world. The Government on its part provides lots of special benefits for woman to bring out her potential to the fore. The challenging and success yearning girls / ladies of the present era wishes to attain success and at the same time give back to the Country (society) that nurtured and motivated her to stand on her own legs The Industrial Revolution in part was fuelled by the economic necessity of many women, single and married, to find waged work outside their home. Women mostly found jobs in domestic service, textile factories, and piece workshops. They also worked in the coal mines. For some, the Industrial Revolution provided independent wages, mobility and a better standard of living. For the majority, however, factory work in the early years of the 19th century resulted in a life of hardship. Women in India have come a long way after independence. From just a skilled homemaker, women today have acquired skills and capabilities of not just being a homemaker but being at par with their male counterparts. This is the new generation of women, who wants to pursue their dream career. But this life is not a bed of roses for all. More conflict arises with the working mother. One has to fulfil the demand at work followed by various demands at home. In today's scenario the husband and wife both work towards creating a balance with their work life as well as at home with their children. But it is still difficult for women as she has to play multiple roles of a cook, a family maid, a tutor, a nurse as well as cater to the demands of office work. This can leave a working woman stressed and anxious; more so if the family is not supportive.

1.2 WHAT IS STRESS?

We live in stressful times. We are holding down two or more jobs. We are putting up with heavy job loads and unreasonable demands. We are swallowing outrage and frustration with unfair situations and irrational superiors because we cannot afford to be laid off or fired. Or we have already been laid off and we are struggling to find another job. Or we have given up and are coping with unemployment. Outside strains like these are called stressors. Stressors are the barely-tolerable pressures that bring us unhappiness and, eventually, disease. Some people hardly seem to be affected by stressors. They maintain a sense of perspective and a sense of humour. They remain calm in the midst of adversity and catastrophe. Other people are overwhelmed by a lesser number and intensity of stressors and slide downhill, losing relationships, jobs, and eventually their mental and physical health. The physiological and psychological responses to situations or events that disturb the equilibrium of an organism constitute stress. While there is little consensus among psychologists about the exact definition of stress, it is agreed that stress results when demands placed on an organism cause unusual

Physical, psychological, or emotional responses. In humans, stress originates from a multitude of sources and causes a wide variety of responses, both positive and negative. Despite its negative connotation, many experts believe some level of stress is essential for well-being and mental health.

Stress in the workplace: a current snapshot The term 'job stress' refers to distress resulting from a situation where the demands of a job are not matched by the resources provided to get the job done. Either or both sides of this equation can be modified to prevent or reduce job stress – modifying demands or stressors and improving job resources. Resources might include a worker's occupational skills, job experience or education, or organizational resources such as machinery, raw materials, or staffing levels available to produce goods or provide services. Job stressors are working conditions that increase the risk of job stress and consequent impacts on health. There are numerous job stress terms, concepts, models and theories, all of which can be understood in the context of the job stress process. The process initiates with exposure to stressors. Stressors arising from the work environment are classified as psychosocial or physical. Psychosocial stressors (also referred to as psychosocial working conditions) include job demands, job control, job insecurity, bullying, harassment and more. Physical stressors include noise and ergonomic exposures (such as awkward working postures and repetitive movements).

Exposure to stressors can lead to perceived distress (strictly speaking, job stress is short for job-related distress). Perceived distress can in turn lead to adverse short-term responses, which can be physiological (e.g. elevated blood pressure), psychological (e.g. tenseness) or behavioral (e.g. smoking or alcohol consumption as forms of coping). Distress, as well as short-term responses, increase the risk of enduring health outcomes of a physiological (e.g. coronary heart disease), psychological (e.g. anxiety disorder) or behavioral (e.g. nicotine addiction, alcoholism) nature. Importantly, job stress can affect health both directly – through neuroendocrine mechanisms and indirectly – through health behavioral pathways. There are three theoretical frameworks, or models, for measuring psychosocial and physical stressors that have been most widely validated and utilized in epidemiological studies of job stress and health. Karasek and Theorell's demand/control model (DCM) is the most widely studied. It postulates that job stress arises from the interaction of low control with high demands which, according to the model produces 'job strain'. Importantly, this model also articulates how work can be health-promoting for workers in jobs with both high demand and high job control (so-called 'active jobs'). Active jobs are both challenging and rewarding.

The health, social and economic impacts of workplace stress The link between workplace stress and quality of work life will adverse effects on physical and mental health has been well substantiated in a large body of international research. Cardiovascular disease (CVD) is the most widely studied physical health outcome. Numerous cross-sectional studies have linked job stress with physiological risk factors for CVD (e.g. hypertension, atherogenic lipids, elevated fibrinogen, overweight/body mass index) and with CVD outcomes (e.g. myocardial infarction, coronary heart disease). Job strain was shown to predict subsequent CVD outcomes after controlling for established CVD risk factors (e.g. smoking, overweight) in more than a dozen prospective cohort studies, including the widely known Whitehall I & II studies. In addition, there is growing evidence that job stress increases the risk of metabolic syndrome and diabetes; this would likely occur through a combination of direct neuroendocrine mechanisms as well as through health behavioural pathways (e.g. low physical activity, poor diet, alcohol consumption). Various measures of job stress, most commonly the demand-control model, have been linked crosssectionally and prospectively to mental health outcomes ranging from increased visits for psychiatric treatment to psychological distress, general mental health, depressive symptoms, major depression, anxiety and suicide. There is a growing number of longitudinal or prospective studies in which measurement of job stressors preceded the development of mental disorders, thus strengthening the confidence with which we can conclude that the increased risk observed is attributable to job stress and not other factors. A 2006 meta-analysis assessed relationships between common mental disorders and various demand-control model measures (job control, job demands, job strain and social support at work) finding in summary robust and consistent evidence that high demands, low control and the combination of the two [job strain] are prospective risks factors for common mental disorders. As well as acting directly through sustained autonomic nervous system activation leading to adverse health impacts, job stress can also harm health indirectly by fostering a range of behaviours which negatively impact on health: cigarette smoking, higher body weight, poor diet, lack of exercise and alcohol abuse. The overall evidence is mixed, but appears strongest for heavy alcohol consumption among men, overweight and the co- occurrence of multiple risky health behaviours.

"Stress is defined as an adaptive response to an external situation that results in physical, psychological and/or behavioral deviations, for organizational participants."

- "Stress is a dynamic condition in which an individual is confronted with an opportunity, constraint or demand related to what he or she desires and for which the outcome is perceived to be both uncertain and important."
- According to Ivancevich and Matterson, 1996 "Stress is the interaction of the individual with the environment. It is an adaptive response, mediated by individual differences and/or psychological process; that is a consequence of any external (environmental) action, situation or event that places excessive psychological and/or physical demands upon a person"
- According to Beehr and Newman, 1998 "Job stress is a condition arising from the interaction of the people and their jobs, and characterized by changes within people that force them to deviate from their normal functioning."

Some important point relating to the nature of stress are:

1. Stress is a neutral word. It is not bad in and of itself. But when stress is created by undesirable outcomes, it becomes Distress. On the other hand, if it is created by desirable and successful effects it is called Eustress. Eustress is a healthy, positive and developmental stress response. It is primarily the Distress form of stress which requires examination and steps to cope with it; because distress is generally associated with heart disease, alchoholism, drug abuse, marital problems, absenteeism etc.
2. Stress is associated with Constraints and Demand. Constraints prevent an individual from doing what he or she desires. If a person wants to buy something, but he does not have the necessary cash, it is a constraint.

Demands refer to the loss of something desired. If a person wants to go and watch a movie, but he is unable to do so because of pressing official work, it amounts to a demand. Both Constraints and Demands can lead to potential stress.

3. Two conditions are necessary for potential stress to become actual stress.

   - Uncertainty over the outcome, and

   - Outcome must be important.

Stress is usually very high when there is uncertainty over the outcome and the outcome is very significant. Both these conditions are necessary. If there is no uncertainty but the outcome is significant, there will not be any stress. On the other hand, if there is uncertainty, but the outcome is not significant, there will again be no stress.

4. Stress is not simply anxiety. Stress may be accompanied by anxiety, but the two are not synonymous. Anxiety is psychological and emotional whereas stress operates in the physiological sphere also along with psychological sphere.

5. Stress should also be differentiated from nervous tension. Nervous tension may be a result of stress. Stress is a subconscious action. Even unconscious people have exhibited stress, whereas nervous tension is a conscious action. People may "bottle up" their emotions and not reveal them through nervous tension.

6. The term "burnout" is also closely associated with stress. Some researchers contend that burnout is a type of stress, but others treat it differently. Burnout is closely associated with helping professions like nursing, education and social work, it is characterized by emotional exhaustion, depersonalization and

diminished personal accomplishments. Even though, technically, burnout is different from stress, these are generally used interchangeably.

Stress is highly individualistic in nature. Some people have high tolerance for stress and thrive well in face of several stressors in the environment. In fact, some individuals will not perform well unless they experience a level of stress which activates and energizes them to put forth their best efforts. On the other hand, some people have very low level of tolerance for stress and they become paralyzed when they have to interface with routine everyday factors that appear undesirable to them.

The workplace stressors predicts serious adverse effects on mental and physical health, even after accounting for other established contributors. Given the widespread prevalence of job stress among working people, this translates to large preventable burdens of common chronic illness and disease. Job stress-related workers' compensation claims statistics substantially underestimate the burden of job stress-attributable common mental disorders, particularly among lower status workers. Job stress is a large and growing public health problem, warranting a commensurate public health response. Feasible and effective intervention strategies are available for addressing job stress in the workplace. The available evidence suggests that priority groups for intervention include younger workers, working women and workers in lower skilled occupations and precarious employment arrangements.

1.3 STRESS MANAGEMENT IN WORK PLACE

People experiencing high levels of stress are more likely to hide the fact than do something about it. The irony is that once the organization is prepared to recognize stress as a business risk, it's relatively straightforward to identify, manage and mitigate – there are tried and tested frameworks and processes available for doing so.

The challenge is in helping your organization to realize that stress is a business risk, and that learning to manage it can have long lasting benefits for the organization.

1.4 QUALITY OF WORK LIFE

Time has transformed from the one when husband used to earn, and the wife remains at home to the time when the husband works and the wife also works outside their homes. But now there is a paradox, wife still cooks food, takes cares of the children and runs the house whereas the husband contributes very little in the household chore. (http://www.indianmba.com). So, making it difficult for her to balance her work with life at home? As time progressed, nuclear families increased. The so called "ideal home" in which the wife used to take care of the home has been faded away. Today's working women are incessantly challenged by the hassle of work and when the day is completed at the workplace, they carry home more of the responsibilities and commitments. The majority of women is working 30-40 hours per week and is under pressure to achieve work-life balance. Their life has become a juggling act that included manifold responsibilities at work and the daily routine tasks of life and home. Effectively creating work-life balance will eventually create more contented employees that contribute to efficiency and success in the place of work. Employers can smooth the progress of WLB with many schemes that can catch the attention of female employees and fulfill their needs which is popularly known as Quality of Work Life.

The impact of stress in working women is more than a male because they have more responsibility and more competition in the environment. The world is globalization and day by day more of innovation to handle in work. Quality of Work Life is the existence of a certain set of organizational condition or practices. This definition frequently argues that a high quality of work life exists when democratic management practices are used, employee's jobs are enriched, employees are treated with dignity and safe working conditions exist. Quality of Work Life refers to the level of satisfaction, motivation, involvement and commitment individuals experience with respect to their lives at work. Quality of Work Life is the degree to which individuals are able to satisfy their important personal needs while employed by the firm. Companies interested in enhancing employees Quality of Work Life generally try to instill in employees the feelings of security, equity, pride, internal democracy, ownership, autonomy, responsibility and flexibility.

1.5 DEFINITION OF QUALITY OF WORK LIFE:

According Lippitt, G.L. (1978) "the term QWL broadly referring to the degree to which work provides an opportunity for an individual to satisfy a wide variety of personal needs to survive with some security, to interact with others, to have a sense of personal usefulness, to be recognized for achievement and to have an opportunity to improve one's skills and knowledge".

Nadler, D. A. and Lawler, E.E. (1983) defined QWL "as an individual's perception of and attitudes towards, his or her work and the total working environment. In simple words, QWL can be defined as an individual's evaluative reactions to satisfaction with his/her work and the total working environment".

Beukema, L. Groningen et al. (1987) expressed that QWL is defined "as the degree to which employees are able to shape their jobs actively, in accordance with their options, interests and needs. It is the degree of power an organization gives to itsemployees to design their work".

Havlovic, S.J. Scobel, D.N et al. (1991) expressed that the QWL "include job security, better reward systems, higher pay, opportunity for growth, and participative groups among others".

Knox, S. and J.A Irving (1997) stated "that the QWL practices and policies of the QWL determine the organization environment, and organization development and interventions operationalise the constructs. Individual employee's perceptions concerning strengths and weaknesses in the total work environment and what is or is not desirable in the workplace are other foci for research".

1.6 EVOLUTION OF QUALITY OF WORK LIFE (QWL)

The Quality of Work Life refers to all the organizational inputs that aim at the employees' satisfaction and enhancing organizational effectiveness. Walton R.E. 2 (1973)1 attributed the evolution of Quality of Work Life to various phases in history. Legislation enacted in early 20th century to protect employees from risks inherent in job and to eliminate hazardous working conditions, followed by the unionization movement in the 1930s and 1940s were the initial steps. Emphasis was on 'job security, due process at the work place and economic gains for the worker'.The 1950s and the 1960s saw the development of different theories by psychologists proposing a positive relationship between morale and productivity, and the possibility that improved human relations that would lead to enhancement of productivity.

1.7 MEANING AND CONCEPT OF QWL

The phrase 'Quality of Work Life' (QWL) connotes different meanings to different people. Some consider it an industrial democracy or co-determination with increased employee participation in the decision making process. For others, particularly managers and administrators, the term denotes improvement in the psychological aspects of work to improve productivity. Unions and workers interpret it as more equitable sharing of profits, job security, healthy and congenial working conditions. Still others view it as improving social relationship at workplace through autonomous work groups. Finally, others take a broader view of changing the entire organizational climate by humanizing work, individualizing organizations and changing the structural and managerial systems. Management considers it as a broader view of changing the entire organizational climate by humanizing work, individualizing organizations, and developing the structural and managerial systems. QWL is the favorableness or unfavorableness of a job environment for people; it refers to the quality of relationship between employees and the total working environment. According to Harrison (1985) 3 , QWL is the degree to which the working organization contributes to material and psychological well-being of its members. The QWL as "a process of joint decision making, collaboration and building mutual respect between management and employees"; it is concerned with increasing labour management co-operation to solve the problems, improving organizational performance and employee satisfaction. According to the American Society of Training and Development (1979), it is a process of work organization which enables its members at all levels to actively participate in shaping the organization's environment, methods and outcomes. This value based process is aimed towards meeting the twin goals of enhanced effectiveness of the organization and improved quality of life for employees.

1.8 THE SCOPE OF WORK LIFE

The issue is complex and difficult to tackle from an organization's perspective because it is different for every individual. The traditional definition of family is a husband who provides financial support, a wife who maintains the household. Cultural differences influence family decisions, and more and more families represent blended racial backgrounds but making work–life integration a way of corporate life is much more difficult. The change in workforce composition 8 has been gradual, but steady. More women are working and, thus, more mothers are in the workforce. In 1996, women comprised46 per cent of the total workforce, compared to 1986 when 44 per cent of the work force was women. Women are less likely to drop-out of the labor force for significant periods of their lives, and more and more women are responsible, alone or with a spouse, for the economic security of their families. The Family and Medical Leave Act, signed by President Clinton in 1993, allowed all US workers to take unpaid leave for up to twelve weeks to care for a seriously ill or new member of the family without putting their jobs at risk. This Act has made the employment picture even more desirables for working mothers, single parents, future parents and two career families. The complex society of ours makes the individuals with conflicting responsibilities and commitments; hence the work-life balance has become a predominant issue at the workplace. The major factors such as the global competition, the renewed interest in personal lives/ family values; and managing the workforce etc. have made it more significant.

1.9 WORK RELATED ISSUES

There are several problems that a woman encounters when she decides to undertake a job in India. The root cause of the problem is the patriarchal structure of the society, where women are expected to give the highest priority to the needs of the family irrespective of whether they work outside the house or not. Their primary role is considered to be looking after the home and children, and their employment outside the home is still regarded as secondary (Arora, 2003). Women's pregnancy and maternity leave might result in a delay in their promotions as compared to their male counterparts. They also face sexual harassment and exploitation in their workplace (Shukla, 2003). When working women try to manage both home and job along with the demands of childcare, they are bound to experience role conflict. One of the greatest drawbacks which resulted from being focused on their career is the high chances of disharmony in their family life, where the modern educated husbands too expect their wives to serve them and the household despite the women working outside the homes. Studies also revealed that the discrimination which a woman faced at the workplace was related to the lower job commitment which was acquired through the socialisation process. When women consider work as an additional role and do not set career goals, they are likely to face problems at work. A low representation of women in higher posts has been considered as a reflection of discrimination in recruitment policies or prejudices as well as the lack of orientation and commitment of women towards their careers. In addition, there are also studies that focused on the changes taking place in women's lives as a result of their employment. Women were able to create a bigger space for themselves by emerging out of the traditional.

1.10 STATEMENT OF THE PROBLEM:

Stress is an inevitable part of everyone's life. There is no denying that stress does have negative effect on the physical and mental health of an individual. Stress within an acceptable limit is required so that an individual will be able to execute the allocated work and responsibility on time. But it depends upon the individual's ability to manage the stress level within the limit. When there is overstress it interferes with the productivity of the individual employee because over stress hampers the thinking capacity of an individual employee, makes him to feel less valued and becomes lazy to work. This over stress can happen due to various reasons which is internal and external to the individual employee's workplace namely, lack of clarity in the job description, cringy relationship with the top management, information overload, monotonous job and so on. Women's contribute a major portion of the workforce and with rapid industrialization their role have become more complex. They are required to cope with the complex career market by enhancing their requisite skills. Due to this demand on the part of the women employees, they experience more conflict and strain **[McLaughlin, Katrina (2003)]**

In view of the above explanation it is found to be significant to undertake a study on impact of the stress on the quality of work life among women employees and offer suggestion to overcome the issue as it has direct negative impact on the productivity and the goodwill of the company.

1.11 NEED FOR THE STUDY

The study on stress and it relationship as well as impact on women employees quality of working life has gained more importance recently due to following reasons,

- Organizations nowadays have become concerned about more than just monetary profit. Employee satisfaction, health, accidents on the job, employee turnover, absenteeism and productivity have been included in a broader evaluation of success and return of investment of the organization.

- It has become crucial to understand the effects of job stress on productivity and performance of employees, such as hospitalization, missing datelines, loss of passion for work and reduced quantity/quality of work. All the said variables positively aid in creating a favorable behavior among the employees towards the organization.

- Job stress if not managed effectively will affect the emotional as well as physical wellbeing of the employee's. The consequences of the stress ,such as absenteeism, decreased productivity, increased healthcare costs may have negative effect on the performance of the organization which may at times affect the good will of the company.

- Today, Quality of Work life (QWL) is viewed as an essential dimension of the quality of life of the employees because intrinsic satisfaction always paves way for better physical wellbeing of the employees. Furthermore high QWL is crucial for the organization to attract and retain best talents in their company.

- Individuals suffer the most when the QWL of the company is not up to the required level. The customers, on whom the profitability of the company is dependent, suffer the most when the QWL of the company is not good.

- The introduction of the new technologies into the field of work nowadays and getting job is narrowed on that account. This forces one to "Not to leave the job" where he finds unsuitable due to work life constraints. All this will pave way for job stress and will have a negative effect on QWL. Understanding about the real usage of new technologies will also help to know about the QWL of the employees.

- When job related issues interact with the employees in a negative manner it will disrupt their physiological and psychological conditions which are surely bound to affect their productivity and final results as well.

- Various studies have revealed that QWL is one of the important parameters which causes negative stress among employees. By emphasizing this factor the areas where the company needs to pay attention can be identified.

- Positive stress is necessary for the better as well competitive performance of the employees. By identifying which job related factor contributes for positive stress, management can pay more attention towards improving and sustaining that job related factor.

1.12 SCOPE OF THE STUDY

The current study has scope in the following areas,

> 1.12.1 By identifying the stress level of the employees, the organization will be able to design, develop and implement employee specific programme's as well initiative's to improve their satisfaction level which will help the management to reduce the negative if any persist among the women employees.

1.12.2 By identifying the problems related to the QWL of the employee's, the management can improve the specific areas where the satisfaction level of the employees are less.

1.12.3 Apart from initiating employee specific stress management progamme, companies will be able to develop policies which will fit the expectations of the employees, from the findings of the study.

1.12.4 This study also serves to identify the job related factors which contributes more towards the achievement of company objective and performance of the employees.

1.12.5 The research can be further used to evaluate the facilities provided by the management towards the employees.

1.12.6 It also helps the management to define additional responsibilities, such as improving the emotional as well as physical wellbeing of their subordinates, involving the subordinates in the decisions related to their work and so on, to the supervisor or the higher officials.

1.12.7 Since women employment has become the symbol of economic viability and social status in modern day society. Therefore organizations through this study will able to find out the specific expectations of the women employees and at the same time they can take steps to improve the same.

1.12.8 Apart from job related factors, other factors like family intrusion in work life, marital stress, gender dis-equality, also influence the women employees negatively and paves way for stress. Through this study company can find out whether the employees are stressed because of job related factors or family intrusion in work life.

1.12.9 Women by nature have the caliber of talking and serving to people with care and empathy. If they are not provided with proper job responsibility matching the said skills, that itself will serve as a source of stress which can be identified through then current study.

1.12.10 The organization will be able to re-design their work structure based on the expectations of the employee.

1.13 OBJECTIVES OF THE STUDY

The objective of the study are as follows:

1. To study the socio-economic status of the working women in Chennai city.
2. To identify and under the underlying dimension of the organization causes of stress (OCS) and personal causes of stress (PCS) variables among working women in Chennai city.
3. To identify and understand the underying dimensions of fulfillment of remedial measures to Reduce stress (FRMRS) variables and quality of work life among working women in Chennai city.
4. To explore the structural influence of stress on Quality of work Life among working women in Chennai.
5. To study the influence of personal profiles, Factor of Organizational Causes of stress (OCS), PERSONAL CAUSES OF STRESS (PCS) and Fulfillment of Remedial measures to reduce stress (FRMRS) on Quality of work life Dimensions.

1.14 CONCLUSION:

This chapter I gives a detailed outline on the theoretical perspective with work stress and how it affects the quality of work life in women's life. Working women could enhance their quality of lives, both in the family as well as work domains. The health, social and economic impacts of workplace stress the link between workplace stress and quality of work life will adversely effects on physical and mental health. Women are still considered responsible for the majority of household labor and management, child care and elder care and employed women work to the equivalent of two full time jobs. (DeMeis & Perkins 1996). This makes employed women experience strain on their time and energy. (Hughes & Galinksy, 1988; Kenney & Bhattacharee, 2000).Research has shown that the more juggling incidents per day, the better her chances for having low satisfaction at the end of the day.(Williams & Suls, 1991) and the chances for experiencing stress buffering effects increases. Next chapter Review of literature which covers the area of Stress, Quality of work life, work life balance.

Chapter II

REVIEW OF LITERATURE

CHAPTER – II

REVIEW OF LITERATURE

2.1 INTRODUCTION:

This Chapter II review of literature where so many authors have published articles on job stress, work life balance, quality of work life. The article covers the area of Stress is the reactions of people which have excessive pressures or other types of demand placed on them. Work stress is explained as the adverse physical and mental reactions that appear when the job demands. Reviews have both Theoretical and conceptual model which helps the study to meet the gaps. However, efforts were also taken to collect information from all available published data, especially from websites, newspapers, magazines and journals.

2.2 INTERNATIONAL STUDIES:

Ambrose Jones, Cynthia P. Guthrie,, Venkataraman M. Iyer, (2012) This study reveals level of stress and out comes which affects the health. They found that women and men perceive same level of stress in the role of ambiguity overload and women has less role conflict. Thus the result of the study it is successful among women in control of stress and turnover.

According to **Adelmann, P. K. (1987).** The study shows the consequence of mental health in specific it speaks about control occupation stress, complexity and personal income. The study shows it bring more happiness and self confidence. The effects of age and education has plays an important role. The regression and occupational character reveals that employed men and women have more happiness and self confidence and not vulnerability.

Chet E. Barney, Steven M. Elias, (2010) This study shows job stress and The objective of this study is to known the negative behavior of employees, flex time and impact of stress on intrinsic and extrinsic motivation. The sate were collected and analyzed well by using multiple regression. It is proven the employee have control on the work environment reduces of job stress.

ChristenMoeller Greg A. Chung-Yan, (2013) The main objective of the study is to find the workplace social support and occupational stress this is known for psychological wellbeing of the professor. The study adopted the multiple regression and the result will be the psychological wellbeing and work place social support. Thus it finds the relationship between the stressor, strains and social support.

Darwish A. Yousef, (2002) The study investigates and explain the potential role of job satisfaction, role of stress, role of ambiguity and other side effective organization, organization commitment and motivation. The author speaks about the positive and negative side of the stressor whish will affect the individual and organization

Edna Rabenu, Aharon Tziner, Gil Sharoni, (2017) The objective of the study is to understand the relationship between the job, work and conflict. On other side organizational justice, organizational citizenship behavior. The study reveals positive on OBC and work family conflict. This study help to know the job related stress and core problem between the family and work.

Elizabeth George, Zakkariya K.A., (2015) The study explains about the job satisfaction and job related stress in different in banking sectors. The author divides into public, private and new generation banks. The job satisfaction and job stress will be different in all three sectors. it shows the wider implication of the service industry.

Emma Donaldson-Feilder and Rachel Lewis (2011) The purpose of this paper is to find the work place stress in line managers. It shows the skills and behaviors which will improve positive stress and reduce the negative as whole. They used different approaches, learning and experience to find the practices and procedures to reduce the stress.

Garima Mathur, Silky Vigg, Simranjeet Sandhar, Umesh Holani, (2007) This study looks at the effect of stress on the performance of the employees working in different manufacturing organizations. In this competitive world companies are facing challenges at every step. Now it has become difficult even to survive in the new economic era. With increased competition work load on the employees has also increased. This study has tried to find out the underlying factors responsible for stress as well as does stress effects the performance of the employees on the job. The result of the study factors such as organizational culture, role and responsibility that are responsible for stress and the regression test has been applied to check the affect of stress on job performance revealed that stress has an effect on job performance and that also a positive affect that is job performance increases with the increase in stress.

Hamed Rashidian, Towhid Pourrostam (2016) In the present competitive world stress plays an important role. The WHO and ILO bring the social and serious which affect the work force health. It state that stress can cause health issues and they have poor life style and less success in life. The root cause of the stress may decrease the efficiency.

According to **Hyo Sun Jung, Hye Hyun Yoon, (2016)** this study shows about the emotional intelligence of the employee and their coping strategy style and job satisfaction among the employee to lead the successful life.

Iram Batool Momina Abid Ruqia Safdar Bajwa (2016) This study reveals that individual and the organization facing multiple issues like stress, motivation and emotional intelligence. The finding are relationship between the emotional intelligence and occupational stress in public and private. Public sector has more emotional intelligence and had more stress compare to other.

Jennifer Walinga, Wendy Rowe, (2017) This paper explore perception of work place stressor and surviving or coping with stress and specific anout the challenges in work place and positive impact like communication strategy,problem solving and congnitive appraisal collaborative and sustainable problem solving, individual learning and growth, and organizational positive impacts. The study provides an original conceptual perspective on the concept of stress management, calling for a paradigm shift that views stress as desirable and conducive to optimal performance.

Jacob Guinot, Ricardo Chiva, Vicente Roca-Puig, (2014) This paper explainsabout the quality of work life and there positive effect and negative effect.Thus it says about the interpersonal trust and positive effect on job satisfaction "Excessive" trust might infer high risk perception, which might increase job stress, and in turn decrease job satisfaction.

Lawrence R. Murphy, Joseph J. Hurrell, Jr, (1987) This study helps to know the work skill and stress management training will reduce the psycho physiological like anxiety, depression and somatic disorder. This study helps to formulate and implement certain program to overcome stress.

Lena Låstad, Tinne Vander Elst, Hans De Witte, (2016) The objective of this paper is to investigate the relationship between individual job insecurity and job insecurity climate over time. Data were collected among readers of a Flemish Human Resources magazine with information from 419 employees working in Flanders. Tool used in the study is correlation a cross-lagged design was used in which both individual job insecurity and job insecurity climate were modeled at all times and reciprocal relationships between these constructs could be investigated. The results showed that perceptions of individual job insecurity were related to perceiving a climate of job insecurity. There is no relationship evidence was found for the effect of job insecurity climate on individual job insecurity. This suggests that job insecurity origins in the individual's perceptions of job insecurity and subsequently expands to include perceptions of a job insecurity climate at the workplace. By investigating the relationship between individual job insecurity and job insecurity climate over time, this study contributes to the understanding of job insecurity, both as an individual and a social phenomenon.

Maria Vakola, Ioannis Nikolaou, (2005) Occupational stress and organizational change are now widely accepted as two major issues in organizational life. The current study explores the linkage between employees' attitudes towards organizational change and two of the most significant constructs in organizational behaviour; occupational stress and organizational commitment. A total of 292 participants completed ASSET, a new "Organizational Screening Tool", which, among other things, measures workplace stress and organizational commitment and a measure assessing attitudes towards organizational change. A limitation of the research design could be that all measures originated from the same source resulting in possible contamination from common method variance. Further, the cross-sectional research design adopted in the present study, as opposed to a longitudinal or experimental methodology, does not allow affirmative causal explanations. The results were in the expected direction showing negative correlations between occupational stressors and attitudes to change, indicating that highly stressed individuals demonstrate decreased commitment and increased reluctance to accept organizational change interventions. The present study showed that good and effective work relationships are very important in organizational change. Handling conflicts, building supportive work relationships and communicating effectively all contribute to the formulation of positive attitudes to change and, therefore, to the success of a change programme. In addition, organizations need to examine the extra workload which organizational change may create. Increase in workload is not only easily attributable to the change but it also makes change unattractive and problematic leading to non-supportive attitudes.

Michael Shane Wood, Dail Fields, (2007) The purpose of this study is to explore the extent to which working in a management team in which leadership functions are shared impacts the role clarity, job overload, stress and job satisfaction of team members. It also aims to explore the moderating influence of organizational encouragement for team work. The study uses data obtained from 200 top management team members working. A model in which role conflict and ambiguity mediate the relationship between shared leadership and job stress and job satisfaction provides the best fit with the data. Shared leadership within a management team was negatively related to team member role overload, role conflict, role ambiguity and job stress. Shared team leadership was positively related to job satisfaction of team members. The relationship of shared leadership with team member job outcomes is stronger in organizations with lower levels of encouragement for teamwork. Although shared leadership within teams may increase job demands on members and require team members to take on new roles, it seems to have positive effects on team member perceptions of their jobs. In addition, the extent to which an organization encourages teamwork makes a difference in the relationship of shared leadership with team member jobs.

Mirjam Haus, Christine Adler, Maria Hagl, Markos Maragkos, Stefan Duschek, (2016) The objective of this paper is to examine specific stressors and demands, perceived control, received support and stress management strategies of crisis managers. Totally, 31 semi-structured interviews with crisis managers were conducted in five European countries and analyzed with the qualitative text analysis method. The sample reported high demands and various sources of stress, including event-specific stressors as well as group specific, occupational stressors such as responsibility for decision making, justification of failures or dealing with press and media. Effective stress management strategies were reported as crucial to ensure successful crisis management, and a need for more comprehensive stress management trainings was emphasized. While stressors and coping strategies in first responders and emergency services personnel have been previously examined, corresponding research regarding the professional group of crisis management leaders remains scarce. Therefore, this study makes an important contribution by examining influential stressors within the work environment of crisis managers and by identifying starting points and requirements for stress management trainings and psychosocial support programs.

Orly Michael, Deborah Court, Pnina Petal, (2009) This research aims to examine the impact of job stress on the organizational commitment of a random, representative sample of coordinators in the Israeli educational mentoring organization. Total population 250 Organizational commitment, including affective, continuance and normative commitment, refers to worker relations in the organization, and how these relations influence the employee's well-being, behavior and contribution to the organization. The study used three questionnaires to investigate the influence of the stress variable and its cumulative effects to predict the coordinators' organizational commitment, among 131 coordinators from six different branches around Israel. Tool used id chi square, correlation. The findings revealed that stress hinders the coordinators' sense of emotional commitment. As the stress level rises, the coordinators' sense of belonging decreases. Another finding was that the stress in the coordinators' job does not influence their overall continuance commitment. Strong continuance commitment was found in two categories: role expectations that were not compatible with the role requirements, and the second, unwillingness to leave the job in the middle of the year. These results could help organizations to better understand the influence of organizational commitment and to manage its implications more effectively. It is suggested that further research should investigate whether those working in educational settings have greater normative commitment than workers in other fields.

Paul Bowen, Peter Edwards, Helen Lingard Keith Cattell (2014) The objective of the study is to relationship between job demands, job control, workplace support, and experiences of stress in the South African construction context is investigated, using hierarchical regression, factor analysis and structural equation modeling to explore the strength of thirteen factor relationships with perceived stress. Data were gathered from an on-line questionnaire survey response sample of 676 architects, civil engineers, quantity surveyors, and project and construction managers. The tool used for the study is correlation analysis and hierarchical regression analysis to test the hypothesis. Predictors displaying a significant relationship with occupational stress are the presence of work–life imbalance, the need to 'prove' oneself, hours worked per week, working to tight deadlines, and support from line managers in difficult situations at work. Existing theories of occupational stress are confirmed but not completely supported. Organizations should look to improving managerial and collegial support for construction professionals, but be careful in engaging in socializing and project team-building activities.

Robert Conti, Jannis Angelis, Cary Cooper, Brian Faragher, Colin Gill, (2006) This empirical paper seeks to address the neglected work condition aspect of lean production (LP) implementation, specifically the relationship between LP and worker job stress. The model incorporates the effects of job demands (physical and psychological), job control and social support. The study employs management and worker questionnaires, management interviews and structured plant tours. The response variable is total worker job stress – the sum of the physical and mental stress levels. The independent variable for the first question is the degree of lean implementation at the sites. The results are based on 1,391 worker responses at 21 sites in the four UK industry sectors. About 11 tested practices are significantly related to stress and an unexpected non-linear response of stress to lean implementation is identified. The regression model shows the scale and significant lean practices of this influence, with the work practices explaining 30 percent of job stress variations. The stress reduction and stress control opportunities identified in the study show the potential for designing and operating effective lean systems while also controlling stress levels. This is the first known multi-industry empirical study of the relationship of job stress to a range of lean practices and to the degree of lean implementation.

Ritsa Fotinatos-Ventouratos, Cary Cooper, (2005) The objective of the study is to findings of a large community wide survey on occupational stress. Data were collected via a questionnaire, using a random sample of the general population in the north east region of England, UK. A total of 2,500 people completed questionnaires, which represented all socio-economic groups. Tool used for the study is chi square and regression The results of the bivariate analysis revealed significant differences in terms of physical and psychological wellbeing amongst the male and female sample. Multiple regression analysis provided evidence that the issue of job satisfaction is critical and different amongst both males and females and social class. The occupational stress can be overcome by proper training and development, prioritizing the work.

Smith, M. Bruyns, S. Evans, (2011) The objective of this paper is to determine how the soft competencies of an information technology (IT) project manager, specifically optimism and stress, can affect project success. The research was exploratory. Experienced IT project managers were requested to relate a "structured" story regarding a significant, personal experience relating to optimism or stress and how this affected the project outcome. In total, eight stories were captured on the optimism theme and five on stress. In total population of 600 employees. Themes from these stories were identified. Qualitative analysis of the stories identified several project managers' optimism themes that strongly influenced IT project success. Tools used for the study is anova and t-test. In addition, it was concluded that IT project success was both positively and negatively influenced by stress. To improve their chances of project success, it was concluded that IT project managers should have a positive but realistic degree of optimism based on a well-accepted project plan. Whilst the project team should expect and embrace stress during the project, this should be carefully managed. Major findings of the study is to improve the training and development program.

Sheena Johnson, Cary Cooper, Sue Cartwright, Ian Donald, Paul Taylor, Clare Millet, (2005) To compare the experience of occupational stress across a large and diverse set of occupations. The total population of the study is 300. Three stress related variables (psychological well-being, physical health and job satisfaction) are discussed and comparisons are made between 26 different occupations on each of these measures. The relationship between physical and psychological stress and job satisfaction at an occupational level is also explored. The measurement tool used is a short stress evaluation tool which provides information on a number of work related stressors and stress outcomes. The tool used for the study is Ranking and correlation. Out of the full ASSET database 26 occupations were selected for inclusion in this paper. – Six occupations are reporting worse than average scores on each of the factors – physical health, psychological well-being and job satisfaction (ambulance workers, teachers, social services, customer services – call centres, prison officers and police). Differences across and within occupational groups, for example, teaching and policing, are detailed. There is little information available that shows the relative values of stress across different occupations, which would enable the direct comparison of stress levels. Major finding of this paper reports the rank order of 26 different occupations on stress and job satisfaction levels.

Sonja Treven, Vojko Potocan, (2005) The purpose of this paper is to present: the problem of stress employees might encounter; To know the individual inclination to stress; To identified the individual methods for reducing stress and the authors' model of training for stress prevention. Total sample size is 250 employees. The paper uses both descriptive and analytical approaches to research and dissemination. Within the descriptive approach various methods are applied, including compilation, descriptive and comparative techniques; the analytical approach involves inductive and deductive methods. Tool used for the study is chi square It emerges that individuals vary considerably in their ability to manage stress. Self-perception, locus of control, type A or B behavioral patterns and flexibility or rigidity, all appear to influence stress management abilities. The organization chooses to assist individuals to manage stress by providing relevant training programs.

Slavyanska V, Dimitrova V, Stankova K (2017) The main objective of the present theoretical research is to demonstrate the necessity and opportunities for stress management in a multi-project environment. It is reached through performance of the following tasks: To identify the stress management as a key factor of project work effectiveness in a multi-project environment; to discuss opportunities for stress management in a multi-project environment. Total population size is 250.Random sampling methods is used for the study, for analysis chi square is used. One of the essential reasons for the unsuccessful realization of the projects in a multi-project environment is the stress provoked by the simultaneous participation in too many projects, each of them having strict restrictions regarding budget, time and quality. Therefore, the management of stress in the project team is an important factor for elaboration of the project work. Fortunately, there exist many possibilities for this.

Terry A. Beehr, John E. Newman (1978) Job stress (and more generally, employee health) has been a relatively neglected area of research among industrial/organizational psychologists. The empirical research that has been done is reviewed within the context of six facets (i.e., environmental, personal, process, human consequences, organizational consequences, and time) of a seven facet conceptualization of the job stress–employee health research domain. (The seventh facet, adaptive responses, is reviewed in the forthcoming second article of this series.) A general and a sequential model are proposed for tying the facets together. It is concluded that some of the major problems of the research in this area are: confusion in the use of terminology regarding the elements of job stress, relatively weak methodology within specific studies, the lack of systematic approaches in the research, the lack of interdisciplinary approaches, and the lack of attention to many elements of the specific facets.

Vathsala Wickramasinghe, (2012) The objective of this study is to examine the moderating effect of supervisor support on the relationship between work schedule flexibility and job stress. For the study a survey methodology was used and 232 software developers attached to offshore outsourced software development firms responded. Tools used is chi square and regression, connivance sampling method is used. It was found that supervisor support moderates the relationship between work schedule flexibility and job stress. The findings of this study will provide useful information for both practitioners and academics to better understand the nature of strategies to be adopted in mitigating job stress.

Yan-Hong Yao, Ying-Ying Fan, Yong-Xing Guo, Yuan Li, (2014) this paper aims to explore the influences of leadership and work stress on employee behavior, the main objective of the study is to know the moderating effects of transactional and transformational leadership on the relationship between work stress and employee negative behavior. Size of the study is 600 Using convenience sampling method, the authors investigated employees from 20 firms in different places and industries, and 347 valid questionnaires were collected. SPSS18.0 statistical analysis software was used for reliability and validity analysis, descriptive statistics, correlation analysis and hierarchical regression analysis to test the hypothesis. The empirical results show that there is a positive correlation between work stress and employee negative behavior. Transformational leadership has negative impacts on work stress and employee negative behavior, whereas transactional leadership has positive influences. Moreover, transactional leadership strengthens the influence of work stress on employee negative behavior, Open leadership is proposed as a new leadership style, which contributes to improving leadership behavior and preventing negative behavior in workplace.

Yitzhak Fried, Kendrith M. Rowland, Gerald R. Ferristhe (2006) There has been considerable growth in the number of studies focused on the relationship between stress at work and a variety of physiological symptoms, especially cardiovascular irregularities, abnormal levels of biochemicals in the blood and urine, and gastrointestinal disorders. Many of these studies, however, have used inadequate procedures for measuring such symptoms. Consequently, the results and conclusions of these studies are often invalid or, at best, questionable. The purpose of this paper is to critique the prevailing procedures used in the measurement of physiological symptoms in work stress research and to suggest needed improvements.

2.3 INDIAN STUDIES

M Aarthy, & M Nandhini (2016) "Influence of the Demographic Factors on Quality of Work Life of the Engineering College Faculty Members in Coimbatore District "in their study The impact of the Quality of Work Life of the faculty members is highly notable and it influences not only the institutions but also the students who are the future building blocks of the nation. The present study concludes that there is a moderate level of Quality of Work Life is found among the faculty members

A. Jayakumar & et. al., (2012) described in his study that there is a direct relationship& indirect relationship between the economic aspects & social well-being of population in which improved QWL aims in improving workers life and his family beyond the limits of industry. The study described the relationship between the QWL & employees with respect to the job satisfaction that involves in maintaining a balanced relationship between work and the family. By imparting education and training, communication and union participation, research projects & adapting in changing environment will enhance in the growth of QWL. The study suggested to take steps that are absolutely necessary to improve the 'Quality of Work Life' by following these tips: Having a personal vision, Test out one's personal own vision, getting trained, finding ways to share their ups and downs with other team workers, sharing the success, taking time for breaks, trying out new ideas, having fun at work. The research concludes that improved QWL not only depends on performance or physical output but also on the workers behavior in solving job related problems that in turn will lead to retain not only the young talents and the new talents but also helps in retaining the existing experience talents.

Kotteeswari , Dr.S.Tameem Sharief (2014), Job stress is negatively related to performance. In other words, higher the stress, lower the performance. Workplace stress derives from many sources. It can be a demanding boss, annoying co-workers. work performance is also affected by stressors such as family relationships, finances , lack of sleep stemming from fears and anxieties about the future. In order to maximize the return on investment organizations are empowering employees to work to their fullest potential. The main objective the factors causing job stress, job stress factors influencing the performance of the employees, coping strategies to overcome stress and improve performance. A sample of 100 employees working in various BPOs in Chennai city. The data are collected by using questioner method. The collected data had been analyzed by chi-square test. 80% of the employees are male and 20% of the employees are female. There is no significant difference in the opinion of the male and female employees regarding their stress in the work place. Both the employer and the employee are following some stress coping strategies to overcome the stress. The employees also can try to overcome their stress through some exercises, yoga and meditation. The employers can extend their support to the employees to get rid of the job stress.

According to **N. A. Krishnamoorthy, M. Vaanmalar QWL (2016)** included aspects that have affected the employees' job satisfaction level and work level which has direct impact on the productivity and the life style of the employees. Therefore, the aspects such as working conditions, personal benefits, health benefits, maternity benefits, wages and insurance benefits and finally, schemes and leave benefits which are major determinants that decides the quality of work of life women employees working in Textile manufacturing industries in Coimbatore are considered in this study. The study confined with only women employees working in textile industries and generally it is observed that the level of awareness is steadily increasing towards the need to empower women through social, economic and political equity, fundamental human rights, improvements in nutrition, basic health and education. The study is exploratory in nature based on structured questionnaire with 720 respondents complying sampling adequacy taking Public Sector and Private Sector Textile Mills selected through proportionate stratified random sampling technique and the samples are collected from 60 textile mills. The study concludes that women are gifted with multitasking abilities and this has become a burden to them due to lean availability work and life space. It is recommended that proper resting and necessary assistance compulsorily needed to enhance the work ability and to achieve the life satisfaction among the women employees particularly women working in Textile Industries considered in this study. When this happens women will become more productive in the work environment and build a happy home.

According to **M. Bhavani and M. Jegadeeshwaran (2014)** Currently employees are considered knowledge workers and what they bring to the world of work in terms of the knowledge and competency matters for the organizations in their desire to be more effective .The present paper aims to study the aspects of job satisfaction and quality of work life among working women teachers in educational institutions coming under University of Mysore. For the purpose of data collection 289 women teachers have been selected using stratified random technique. The questionnaire has three sections. First section is related to various socio-economic or demographic variables of the respondents, second section consists of fifteen items to measure the job satisfaction level of women teachers by using Likert's four point scale and third section consists of 34 items to measure quality of work life through Likert's five point scale. The tools used for the study are ANOVA, Chi square. The data was collected during the January 2013 to June 2013.The present study aims to understand the relationship between job satisfaction on quality of work life. The result of the study shows that there is positive impact of job satisfaction on quality of work life of women teachers.

Malavika Desai, Bishakha Majumdar, Tanusree Chakraborty, Kamalika Ghosh, (2011) The study aims to establish the effect of personal resourcefulness and marital adjustment on job satisfaction and life satisfaction of working women in India. A total of 300 women are studied – 100 each in the working women, home-based working women, and homemakers categories – using the following scales: socio economic status scale, general health questionnaire, self-esteem inventory, life satisfaction scale, perceived stress scale, marital adjustment scale, the self-control schedule, and job satisfaction questionnaire. It is found that the home-based working women are the least stressed, most well adjusted, and the most satisfied with their careers among the groups studied. Their ways of perceiving and handling stress are found to be more effective than those used by women in the other two groups. The study implicates women friendly work policies – like flexible job hours and home office – as well as a cooperative home environment and assistance for housework. Stress relief programmes, yoga and an overall change of attitude towards housework, female employees and sex roles are needed.

Manjunatha M K., and T.P.Renukamurthy. (2017) The aim of this research is to understand roots and outcomes of job stress on the employee performance in banking sector For banking employees around the globe, stress on the job can be a challenge; stress can be sometimes positive and sometimes negative. Positive stress leads to productivity and negative stress leads to loss for the organization. The population of the study is 300.They adopted random sampling method. Tools used is chi square and ANOVA The major findings of the study there is significant relationship between the stress and well being of the employees. Stress can make an individual, productive, constructive and well managed Positive attitude and meditation will be helpful for coping the stress. There are various ways for managing stress, such as Breathing exercises, Progressive relaxation, Stretching exercise, Walking and Sleeping. Hence, it will be successful if it makes distress. It enhance the psychological well-being and health of the employees

Mini Amit Arrawatia1, Deepanshi (2017) The main purpose of this research to focus on the private sector banks employees because banking employees are very stressed. They are highly target driven and also face high work pressure. The study has been conducted on 200 employees including private banks managers and employees; The three major objectives of the study is to find the main causes of stress among private bank employees, To recognize the effects of stress on the health issues. To analyze the impact of stress on the performance of employees and examine the relationship of stress and performance. They are randomly selected from different branches of private banks. 220 questionnaires were distributed out of which 156 employees responded. The present study is descriptive in nature. For analysis purpose data Reliability, Validity, correlation test are been used to find out relationship between stress and employees performance. and regression analysis also used. The study shows large number of respondent's suffers from headache & weakness. There is positive correlation between stress and performance of the employees. Similarly lack of motivation, lack of management support have positive correlation with stress of the employees. The study also showed that there is a negative correlation between lack of cooperation with superior, long working hours and also studied that technical problem, work environment into employees performance. This study recognized the health problem of employees because stress also gives negative impact of employee's health.

Mohajan, H.K. (2012) This paper is about occupational stress and management of this type of stress. Recently occupational stress is increasing due to globalization and global economic crisis which is affecting almost all countries, all professions and all categories of workers, as well as families and societies. Total population of the study is 400 and connivances sample method is used. Many organizations want to reduce and prevent the employee stress because they observe that it is a major drain on corporate productivity. The paper also discusses the risk management at work place, prevention of stress and tips to stress management. Values of s C are obtained by calculating the coefficient of correlation between the stressors and stress outcomes, r and then converting r into r^2, and then converting the value of r^2 into percent. We have observed that nobody is free from stress, everybody under the stress a little bit or more. A major finding of the study stress are not harmful but over stress is harmful and creates many diseases. We have discussed both the positive and negative sides of stress. Occupational stress is become an essential factor in the worldwide due to competition among the nations to face economic crisis.

Nandhini, M. Usha, P. Palanivelu (2016) The objective of the study is to find the causes of stress, stress level on employees, To known the effect of stress on productivity of an organization .To study the effect of stress on personal growth. To identify stress coping strategies at organizational level. The research design used in the study is Descriptive research design. Using the random sampling method the data were collected from 150 employees. The analysis is done through Percentage analysis, Chi-square test. Majority of the respondents agrees that work stress interferes and upset their family life. There is significant relationship between age and reason for stress among employees. There is significant relationship between Monthly income and impact of stress in work place. The study shows the company should provide proper career development and performance appraisal will encourage the employee to excel and free from stress.

Nasreen Zehra and Riffat Faizan (2017) This paper discusses the stress management impacts on the employee performances at workplace. The objective of the study if to find the stress control's role in increasing employee motivation and overall satisfaction in project based organizations. Survey questionnaire and open- ended interviews are primary instruments used in this study. Total 112 employees participated in survey questionnaire while total 26 managers were interviewed. Tools used for the study is Chi square. Findings revealed that unrealistic demands generate stress at workplace. Interestingly, we found traditional assumption of pay scale creating stress is opposed as 57% respondents have content with the pay scale thus pay scale is not the fundamental factor for generating stress. The stress exists and operates in both micro and macro environment having equally significant impact on individuals. Their respective performance hinder due to decline in the working efficiency and quality work. we found that there is no relation between work-life balance is not effective in stress reduction but act as additional stressor for employees under chronic stress.

Prakash B. Kundaragi (2015) "Stress is nothing more than a socially acceptable form of mental illness". Stress has been defined in different ways over the years. The objective of the study was conceived of as pressure from the environment, then as strain within the person. Today is one of interaction between the situation and the individual. It is the psychological and physical state that results when the resources of the individual are not sufficient to cope with the demands and pressures of the situation. Total population of 350 employs. Method of sampling adopted is random method. There is no significant relationship between the Negative stresses or Distress kills the employees' positive attitude and it turns to absent, turnover, immoral, anxiety, depression, aggressive and so on. Hence, we will be successful if we make distress into eu-stress, our healthy lifestyle as well as organizational well being will change.

PratibhaGoyal Zahid Nadeem (2004) The study is about stress among women Data from a micro survey of women executives in Ludhiana shows that women are becoming more and more career conscious, they want to take up challenging roles for growth and development, so wherever they are considered in the stereotyped framework, they face stress. The total population of the study is 300. Random sampling method is chosen. Tools used for the study is correlation . Therefore their going to the workplace is very much accepted by family members. Major findings Due to this acceptance, other family members try to adjust their roles within the family and a change is being felt in the attitude of the husband and other family members. Moreover due to changes in the technological environment, telecommunication, better transportation facilities, electronic gadgets etc., stress is reduced.

P.V.Pothigaimalai & R.Buvaneshwari (2014) stated that the personal needs of any members working in the organization can be achieved only by having prior experience and through sense of satisfaction towards his job. It aims in creating a healthy environment where employees can work cooperatively and achieve organizational results effectively. The study gives clear picture about various dimensions like providing fair compensation, safe working environment, and opportunity for growth, work and personal life that ensures dignity to the employees in an organization. The research is done logically to identify the QWL of employees and suggest various possible methods in improving QWL. The sample size is 90. The study is carried out by adopting Descriptive, Exploratory and Diagnostic designs for research methodology. Simple Random sampling Technique of probability sampling method was used by the researcher. The data was analyzed by applying percentage analysis, Chi- Square test and Anova. It is recommended to organization to provide all amenities to the employees that make them feel motivated and happy.

Radha Damle (2016) The objective of the study to study the performance of employees as a function of occupational stress and coping. To study occupational stress in relation with coping of central government employees. To study occupational stress of central government employees with respect to occupational level, gender and age group. The sampling technique followed was stratified random sampling based on the proportion of officers and staff in the population. The required sample size was 206. ANOVA, correlation, t- statistic was conducted to explore different relationships Analysis of the occupational stress level indicated low to moderate stress at work. Majority of employees, ninety one percent, perceived moderate stress. Importantly, not a single employee reported to experience of high stress Gender difference in coping was observed only for cognitive avoidance coping strategy. Female employees used this strategy more than male employees. This study concludes that performance of central government employees is influenced by occupational stress and effort expended by them in coping with stress. Central government employees are not a stress free community. Overall similarity in coping behavior of employees is indicative of a possibility that the bureaucratic structure has an important role to play in deciding the reactions of employees.

Rochita Ganguly (2010) conducted study to know the relationship between quality of work life and job satisfaction among university employees. The result of the study reveals that the university employees were not happy with the degree of autonomy they are enjoy- ing, the nature of personal growth opportunities, work complexity, their control on the task and the degree of top management support in the work. The study also reveals that there is positive relationship between job satisfaction and QWL. Ayesha Tabassum (2012) used Walton's eight components of quality of work life to measure the relationship between the components of QWL and job satisfaction in faculty members of private universities in Bangladesh. The study reveals that all the components are positively associated with the job satisfaction of faculty.

Sathyanaraynan, Dr. K. Maran (2011) The objective of the study is to understand the job stress and its impact. To identifies the relationship between job stress and work environment, To know the relationship between stress and gender Descriptive research is been adopted for the study, which includes surveys and fact finding enquiries of different kinds. The total sample size for the study was 150. Convenience sampling method is used for the study. The data is collected through Interview schedule. SPSS tool is used to find the correlation between various stressors .T test is used to find the gender variability and frequency table is been used. Major factors contributing to stress Workload, Vulnerability, Low Physical Condition. There is significant correlation between Workload and Emotional Exhaustion. There is no significant difference in stress variable with reference to gender. The company can concentrate on providing some stress relief program which helps them to reduce the stress level. The employees are satisfied with the company environment and they are working with the medium stress level in the organization.

Shobana.S Chacko nisha., Verma Rekha and Mathur anjali (2016) It is an important task for working women to balance responsibilities both at work place and at home. This challenging task causes stress at different level in working women's life. The aim of the study is to focus on the stress causes among government and private working women with the objective to compare the occupational stress level between women's working in government and private sector. Socio Economic Status Scale devised are used. A sample of 180 working women, out of this 90 each from government and private sector are participated in this study. The 90 working women from each sector are further divided into three categories of lower, middle and upper socio-economic group comprising 30 samples in each group. Statistical test and two-way ANOVA were used for data analysis. The finding of the study reflects that there was a significant difference in stress level between working women in government and private sectors.

Tulsee Giri Goswami, Richa Burman (2015) Man is a social animal and society is what makes or breaks a human. This is especially true in a society like India where policing plays an important role. As a general rule, work is considered as one of the most important functioning of human life and has a great impact on individual overall well-being. The issues which cause problem are like police force has to perform risky assignments, working hours are comparatively long, rigid hierarchy pattern and along with this policemen have to maintain law and order in the state as well. Such situation cause stress at work and creates impact on work place outcome like the level of job satisfaction and psychological wellbeing. The major objective of the study is To find out the impact of work stress on job satisfaction among police officers. To find out the impact of job stress on psychological wellbeing among police officers. Using the random sampling method, the data were collected from 150 employees. The collected data were analyzed by employing the statistical tools like Percentage analysis, Chi-square test, This study has been successful in identifying the impact of work stress on job satisfaction and psychological well-being. It can be concluded that occupational stress is a major issue in the work-related safety and health aspect and plays a vital role in on police officers life. The work stress is associated with poor psychological and emotional health and high job dissatisfaction the result of this study proves that workplace support is considered as avenues to increase job satisfaction among the police officers. Therefore, it is recommended to reduce the stressful conditions and to improve job satisfaction.

V Sumathi, & R Velmurugan (2017) Quality of work life is a critical concept with having lots of importance in employee's life. A high quality of work life (QWL) is essential for all organizations to continue to attract and retain employee. This study attempted to find out the factors that have an impact and influence on quality of work life of employees in private limited companies of Coimbatore. The research design chosen is descriptive in nature. The sample size taken to conduct the research is 175 employees in private companies the respondents were selected by using convenient sampling technique. Structured interview schedule was used for primary data collection. Secondary data was collected from earlier research work. Simple Percentage Analysis, Rank correlation and Weighted Average method Analysis are the tools used for data analysis. In order to have a greater and effective quality of work life the private companies must fulfill and need to go extra mile in order that the employee can retained with least effort and can provide the best results to the company. The success of any organization depends on the efficiency of labour are increasing the efficiency. The organization promote of Quality of work life in the employees.

Xavior Selvakumar & S. Lawrence Immanuel (2015) The job stress is an increasing problem in present day organizations; it does not affect the employees work life only, but has far reaching impact on employees' family life as well. Stress refers to the pressure or tension people feel in life. The total sample size of 160 respondents comprising of 80 branches of SBI were taken for the study. Both descriptive and explanatory research methodologies are adopted in this study. As such, self-administered standardized questionnaire is used to gather all relevant information on the subject matter. The study is descriptive in nature and Normative Survey method is chosen by the researcher. The researcher had chosen the stratified random sampling method for the present study. Under stratified sampling the population is divided into three sub-populations that are individually more homogeneous than the total population which are called stratums and then to select items from each stratum to constitute a sample. There is significant relation between the work stress and family life. Therefore, it is recommended to reduce the stressful conditions and to improve job satisfaction more attention should be given on the roles and the support that they receive.

2.4 CONCLUSION:

This chapter II has covered the area of job stress, Quality of work life, work life balance of working women. Stress is described as a worst condition of emotions in terms of physiological rise when people experience a negative situation in such a way that they perceive a danger to their prosperity. In line with the studies depicted in this chapter it is clearly evident that stress does have an impact on the quality of working life of the employees **[Mirjam Haus**

et al (2016), Paul Bowen et al (2014)]. The review of related studies has paved way for proper breaking down of variables for the study and also edifies to weigh the study on the conceptual framework that is understood by the reviews. Further, this chapter showcased that not much studies based on women employees were undertaken and gives a clarity to narrow down the topic based on the gap so identified from the constructive review of various recent studies [**Krishnamoorthy & Vaanmalar (2016), Malavika Desai et al (2011)].** In next chapter we will discuss the research methodology used in detail.

Chapter III

RESEARCH METHODOLOGY

CHAPTER - III

RESEARCH METHODOLOGY

3.1 INTRODUCTION:

The way through which research problem under study is systematically solved is said to be research methodology. This chapter shows in detail the various steps that is adopted for studying the research aim in question. In addition, it also mentions the sampling design used, the statistical tools used for breaking down the raw data and analyzing the same. The present study is analytical in nature and has adopted survey method for its findings. This study is based mainly on the primary data collected from the employees working in Public and Private sector employees the through a well-designed and well- structured questionnaire. However, efforts were also taken to collect information from all available published data, especially from websites, newspapers, magazines and journals.

3.2 RESEARCH DESIGN, SAMPLING SIZE AND DESIGN

The design of research that is adopted for the study is descriptive, which means the response collected and reported as it is without any act of manipulation. The convenient random sampling method has been adopted to collect primary data from the working women. A total of 1,000 copies of the well-designed structure questionnaire were distributed in Chennai city. The data were collected from March 2018 to December 2018. After giving adequate time to the respondents 788 filled in questions were received. On scrutiny, 102 incomplete questioners were identified and 62 questionnaires were found to be unsuitable for the study because of their extreme values. The remaining 624 questionnaire were considered for the study. The study period was 2015 to 2019.

3.3 QUESTIONNAIRE DESIGN AND SCALING PATTERN

A questionnaire with **Five - Sections** was finalized to collect information from the Information sector employees.

Section I is about profiles of the respondents such as age, marital status, educational qualification, total number of work experience in current organisation, total number of working hours per day, nature of family, monthly income, nature of organisation and level of employment.

Section II has 23 aspects of Organisational Causes of Stress (OCS) variables.

Section III has 8 aspects of Personal Causes of Stress (PCS) Variables.

Section IV has 15 aspects of fulfillment on Remedial Measures to Reduce Stress (RMRS) variables

Section V has 20 aspects of Quality of Work Life (QWL) variables.

OCS, PCS, RMRS and QWL variables have been measured using 5 point Likert scale of 5,4,3,2 and 1 for their responses of Strongly agree, Agree, Undecided, Disagree and Strongly disagree respectively.

3.4 MEASUREMENT OF VARIABLES AND SCALING PATTERN

3.4.1 Nominal Scale: The personal profile variables of the male consumers such as, age, marital status, educational qualification, and nature of family, monthly income, nature of organisation and level of employment are measured in appropriate nominal scale.

- **3.4.2 Ratio Scale:** Total number of work experience in current organisation and total number of working hours per day are also measured in the appropriate ratio scale.
- **3.4.3 5 Point Likert Scale:** The opinion of the working women about each variable of Organisational Causes of Stress (OCS), Personal Causes of Stress (PCS) Variables, Quality of Work Life (QWL) and Remedial Measures to Reduce Stress (RMRS) has been measured in 5 point Likert scale of strongly agree, agree, undecided, disagree and strongly disagree with the weightage of 5,4,3,2 and 1 respectively.

3.5 ANALYSIS OF DATA

The primary data collected were subjected to statistical analysis using SPSS version 21.0.

- **3.5.1 Percentage Analysis** has been used to understand personal profiles of the working women and Descriptive statistics has been used to identify the total experience and working hours per day among working women.

- **3.5.2 Factor Analysis** has been applied to identify the underlying- latent dimensions of the variables of Organisational Causes of Stress (OCS), Personal Causes of Stress (PCS) Variables, Quality of Work Life (QWL) and Remedial Measures to Reduce Stress (RMRS) among working women.

- **3.5.3 Descriptive statistics** has been used to understand the characteristics of Organisational Causes of Stress (OCS), Personal Causes of Stress (PCS) Variables, Quality of Work Life (QWL) and Remedial Measures to Reduce Stress (RMRS) factors and its distributions.

- **3.5.4 T-test and F-test** have been applied to find out the significance of difference/s between various personal profiles of the working women with Organisational Causes of Stress (OCS), Personal Causes of Stress (PCS) Factors.

3.5.5 Cluster Analysis has been used to identify the dominant groups of respondents differentiated significantly by the factors of OCS, PCS and QWL and

3.5.6 Discriminant analysis has also been used to validate the cluster classification.

3.5.7 The multiple regression analysis has been run to find out the significant factors that influence Quality of Work Life among working women.

3.5.8 Structural Equation Model (SEM) has been applied to explore the structural effect of stress dimensions on quality of work life among working women.

3.6 PILOT STUDY AND PRE-TESTING

A pilot study was conducted with a sample of 50 questionnaires. The results were subjected to Cronbach alpha test for checking the internal consistency and reliability of the scale. The values obtained were as follows:

Table 3.6.1

Scale reliability of Stress and QWL variables

Variables	No. of statements	Alpha co-efficient
Organisational Causes of Stress (OCS)	23	0.901
Personal Causes of Stress (PCS)	8	0.864
Fulfillment of Remedial Measures to Reduce Stress (FRMRS)	15	0.919
Quality of Work life	20	0817

The table 3.6.1 shows that Cronbach's alpha values for all types of variables were high

(Above 0.750). Therefore, there is high consistency in measurement of the different types of variables and the scaling is highly reliable. However, in the light of experience gained through pilot study, the questionnaire was modified to elicit responses from the sample group.

3.7 CONCLUSION:

The current chapter has given clarity on the methodology and stages through which the research work progressed. The primary data collected were subjected to statistical analysis using SPSS version. Percentage Analysis, Factor Analysis, Descriptive statistics, T-test and F-test, Cluster Analysis, Discriminant analysis, multiple regression analysis, Structural Equation Model (SEM) are used. The next chapter is devoted to data analysis and interpretation.

Chapter IV

ANALYSIS AND INTERPRETATION

CHAPTER – IV

DATA ANALYSIS AND INTERPRETATION

4.1 INTRODUCTION

The following chapter explains about the stress level of women employees in the Chennai city. In this chapter the attempt has been made to identify the different dimensions of personal causes of stress, organisational causes of stress and coping strategies to reduce stress and quality of work life of women employees in the Chennai city. Further, this chapter explored the structural influence of stress on quality of work life of women employees in the study area. The primary data collected were subjected to Percentage analysis, Factor analysis, Independent Sample t test, Analysis of Variance (ANOVA), Multiple Regression, Cluster analysis, Discriminant analysis and structural equation model has been applied through SPSS Version. 23.0.

4.1.1 Personal Characteristics of the Women Employees

The percentage analysis has been applied to understand the personal characteristics of the women employees participated in the primary survey. The personal characteristics of women employees residing in the Chennai city has been presented in the Table 1.

The **Personal characteristics of the women employees** identified are as follows:

1. Age
2. Educational Qualification
3. Monthly Income
4. Area of Living
5. Nature of family
6. Marital Status

Table 1: Personal Characteristics

Personal Characteristics (Total No. of Respondents = 624)	Frequency	Percent
Age		
Between 20 to 30 Yrs	215	34.5
Between 31 to 40 Yrs	256	41.0
Between 41 to 50 Yrs	97	15.5
Above 51 Yrs	56	9.0
Educational Qualification		
School Level	76	12.2
Graduate	167	26.8
Post – Graduate	248	39.7
Professional	110	17.6
Others	23	3.7
Monthly Income (In Rs.)		
Below Rs. 20,000	156	25.0
Rs.20,001 – Rs.40,000	312	50.0
Rs.40,001 – Rs.60,000	123	19.7
Above Rs.60,001	33	5.3
Area of Living		
Urban	345	55.3
Semi – Urban	279	44.7
Nature of Family		
Nuclear Family	401	64.3
Joint Family	223	35.7
Marital Status		
Married	405	64.9
Unmarried	219	35.1

Age: The demographic characteristics of the result explored that the age groups such as most of the respondents aged between 31 to 40 years group (41.0%) and followed by other age groups with respect in order frequency 20 to 30 years age group (34.5%), 41 to 50 years (15.5%) and above 51 years (9.0%).

Educational Qualification: The result of education qualification level among respondents revels that the most of them post graduates (PG) (39.7%) followed by under graduates (UG) (26.8%), professionals (17.6%), school level (12.2%) and other educational qualification (3.7%).

Monthly Income (In Rs.): The results of monthly income of the respondent explored that most of them earning Rs.20,000 to Rs.40,000 (50.0%) followed by, below Rs.20,000 (25.0%), Rs.40,001 to Rs.60,000 (19.7%) and Above Rs.60,001 (5.3%).

Area of Living: The Majority of the respondents are living in urban area (55.3%) and followed by semi-urban area (44.7%).

Nature of the Family: The majority of the respondents is hailing from the nuclear family (64.9%) and followed by joint family of the respondents (35.1%).

Marital Status: The result explores that the majority of the respondents are married (64.9%) and followed by unmarried (35.1%).

Employment Characteristics of the Women Employees

The percentage analysis and descriptive statistics has been applied to understand the employment characteristics of the women employees participated in the primary survey. The employment characteristics of women employees residing in the Chennai city has been presented in the Table 2.

The **employment characteristics of the women employees** identified are as follows:
1. Nature of Organisation
2. Schedule of Work
3. Level of employment
4. Experience (Years)
5. Working Hours per day

Table 2: Employment Characteristics

Employment Profile (N = 624)	Frequency	Percent
Nature of Organisation		
Private Sector	514	82.4
Public Sector	110	17.6
Schedule of Work		
Day Shift	319	51.1
Night Shift	133	21.3
Rotational Shift	172	27.6
Level of Employment		
Low Level	188	30.1
Middle Level	294	47.1
Higher Level	142	22.8
Descriptive Statistics		
	Experience (In Years)	Working Hours Per Day (In Hrs)
Mean	7.90	8.37
Std. Deviation	4.421	1.450
Minimum	1	3
Maximum	33	18

Nature of Organisation: The majority of the respondents is working in private sector (82.4%) organisations and followed by public sectors (17.6%).

Schedule of Work: The majority of the respondents is their work schedule are day shift (51.1%) followed by, rotational shift work schedule (27.6%) and night shift work schedule (21.3%).

Level of Employment: The empirical result explores that the sizeable portion of the respondents are working in middle level (47.1%) designations followed by low level designations (30.1%) and higher level designations (22.8%).

Experience (In Years): The descriptive statistics proves that average experience of the respondents is 7.90 years with the standard deviation value of 4.421 years

Working Hours Per Day (In Hrs): The descriptive statistics proves that average working hours per day is 8.37 hours with the standard deviation value of 1.450.

EXPLORATORY FACTOR ANALYSIS – FACTORS INFLUENCING CAUSES OF STRESS AND QUALITY WORK LIFE

The exploratory factor analysis were used to analyse the data reduction with respect to summaries a number of constructs into a smaller set of composite dimensions. This technique is an important step in construct development and can be used to demonstrate, construct validity of scale items and sampling adequacy level. In this part of the analysis the attempt has been made to determine the dimensions to influencing the causes of stress and quality work life of the women employees. The constructs are quoted in a structured survey instruments and the items were obtained from the existed literatures. Therefore the data reduction is done through the application of exploratory factor analysis by principal component method with varimax rotation and the following results are obtained.

ORGANISATIONAL CAUSES OF STRESS

The common causes of stress at workplace due to excessive workloads, lack of concentrations, lack of interpersonal support, lack of monetary benefits and non-monetary benefits and poor working environment etc., are organisational causes of stress or organisational stressors. Exploratory factor analysis on twenty three items of organisational causes stress yielded into two dimensions which accounted for 63.153% of the total variance with the total of 14.525 Eigen value, 0.960 Kaiser- Mayer-Olkin measure of sampling adequacy value (KMO). This indicates that the meritorious level of prediction. The significance level of Bartlett's Test of Sphericity (BTS) was 0.000, which means that the data are appropriate for factor analysis. The result of the KMO and BTS tests show that the data meet the fundamental requirements of factor analysis. The overall cronbach's alpha co-efficient were 0.967 which is considered as good level. The factor loadings ranged from 0.545 to 0.806 and the factor extracted were labelled based on the items loaded. The table were presented below

Table 3: Exploratory Factor Analysis – Organisational Causes of Stress

Particulars	Mean (SD)	Communalities	Variance (Eigen Value)	Reliability	Loadings
Job Description Factor			33.509 (7.707)	0.952	
Lack of Role Clarity (OCS1.20)	3.56 (1.294)	0.716			0.785
Lack of Training & Development (OCS1.19)	3.53 (1.241)	0.686			0.775
Lack of Participation in Decision-making (OCS1.22)	3.49 (1.312)	0.690			0.752
Lack of Counseling (OCS1.18)	3.48 (1.350)	0.653			0.749
Lack of Management/Peer Support (OCS1.21)	3.53 (1.232)	0.626			0.735
Lack of Career Development Opportunities (OCS1.14)	3.40 (1.281)	0.624			0.699

Improper Salary structure (OCS1.10)	3.62 (1.250)	0.670		0.656
Maternity and Paternity leave not sanctioned fully as per Rules (OCS1.23)	3.47 (1.246)	0.581		0.647
Innovation and Creativity is not Encouraged (OCS1.17)	3.43 (1.264)	0.577		0.627
Improper Grievance handling mechanism (OCS1.12)	3.59 (1.272)	0.565		0.610
Comparing the Performance with Other Employees (OCS1.16)	3.54 (1.288)	0.590		0.603
Unsafe Working Environment (OCS1.9)	3.51 (1.232)	0.612		0.579
Frequent Changes in Responsibility/Authority (OCS1.11)	3.49 (1.230)	0.604		0.558
Inadequate infrastructure to do the job properly (OCS1.13)	3.53 (1.249)	0.560		0.545
Job Structure Factor			**29.644 (6.818)**	**0.928**
Poorly Motivated (OCS1.3)	3.46 (1.344)	0.718		0.806
Lack of Concern for employee health and well-being (OCS1.2)	3.42 (1.266)	0.713		0.799
Less of Salary/Wages/Compensation (OCS1.4)	3.53 (1.326)	0.697		0.716
Excessive Work Load (OCS1.5)	3.44 (1.292)	0.634		0.698
Long Working hours and Overtime (OCS1.6)	3.55 (1.280)	0.669		0.682
Job Insecurity (OCS1.1)	3.27 (1.404)	0.546		0.676
Unclear Policies and Procedures (OCS1.15)	3.53 (1.188)	0.599		0.647
Lack of Proper communication channel (OCS1.7)	3.53 (1.267)	0.601		0.645
Lack of Concentration in Planning (OCS1.8)	3.52 (1.297)	0.595		0.559

Total Variance 63.153% ; Cronbach's Alpha Value = 0.967 (23 Items)

KMO and Bartlett's Test - Kaiser-Meyer-Olkin Measure of Sampling Adequacy. = 0.960
(Bartlett's Test of Sphericity Approx. Chi-Square = 11381.993; df = 253; Sig. = 0.000)

Job Description Factor: Job description is enlightening credentials of the objectives, responsibilities, assignments, responsibilities and working conditions related to the job listing in the organization through the process of job analysis. Job Description also details the talents, potential and skills with required qualifications that an individual applying for the job execution. The factor loadings ranged from 0.545 to 0.785 with the variance of 33.509% and 7.707 eigen value. the items loaded under this factor are

Lack of Role Clarity (OCS1.20), Lack of Training & Development (OCS1.19), Lack of Participation in Decision-making (OCS1.22), Lack of Counseling (OCS1.18), Lack of Management/Peer Support (OCS1.21), Lack of Career Development Opportunities (OCS1.14), Improper Salary structure (OCS1.10), Maternity and Paternity leave not sanctioned fully as per Rules (OCS1.23), Innovation and Creativity is not Encouraged (OCS1.17), Improper Grievance handling mechanism (OCS1.12), Comparing the Performance with Other Employees (OCS1.16), Unsafe Working Environment (OCS1.9), Frequent Changes in Responsibility/Authority (OCS1.11) and Inadequate infrastructure to do the job properly (OCS1.13). Based on this items the dimension has been labeled as **"Job Description Factor"**.

Job Structure Factor: Job structure was used by organisation to outline an overall hierarchy and reporting structure for each job within the organization, and also defines, educates and enumerates how an organization will work in order to meet its short term and long term goals. The factor loadings ranged from 0.559 to 0.806 with the variance of 29.644% and 6.818 Eigen value. the items loaded under this factor are Poorly Motivated (OCS1.3), Lack of Concern for employee health and well-being (OCS1.2), Less of Salary/Wages/Compensation (OCS1.4), Excessive Work Load (OCS1.5), Long Working hours and Overtime (OCS1.6), Job Insecurity (OCS1.1), Unclear Policies and Procedures (OCS1.15), Lack of Proper communication channel (OCS1.7) and Lack of Concentration in Planning (OCS1.8). Based on this items it has been labeled as **"Job Structure Factor"**.

Table 4

Descriptive Statistics

Description	Mean	Std. Deviation	Skewness		Kurtosis	
			Statistic	Std. Error	Statistic	Std. Error
Job Description Factor	49.1587	13.91082	-0.480	0.098	-0.835	0.195
Job Structure Factor	31.2580	9.29967	-0.559	0.098	-0.847	0.195
Organisational	**80.4167**	**22.40069**	**-0.487**	**0.098**	**-0.900**	**0.195**

The table 4 shows that out of maximum value of 70 *(5x14 **JDF** variables)*, the mean value of 49.1587 is a robust measure of **JDF** as the standard deviation is lower. The **JDF** distribution has a slight negative skewness. Out of maximum value of 45 *(5x9 JSF variables)*, the mean value of **31.2580** is a robust measure of **JSF** as the standard deviation is lower. The **JSF** distribution has a slight negative skewness. Out of maximum value of 115 *(5x23 OCS variables)*, the mean value of 80.4167 is a robust measure of OCS as the standard deviation is lower. The OCS distribution has a slight negative skewness.

Table 5

Test of Normality

Description	Kolmogorov-Smirnov[a]			Shapiro-Wilk		
	Statistic	Df	Sig.	Statistic	Df	Sig.
Job Description Factor	0.126	624	.000	0.931	624	.000
Job Structure Factor	0.148	624	.000	0.924	624	.000
Organisational Causes of Stress	0.124	624	.000	0.926	624	.000

a. Lilliefors Significance Correction

Table 5 indicates that the by Kolmogorov-Smirnov Test of normality (Statistic Value = 0.124, P-Value = 0.000) and Shapiro-Wilk Test of Normality (Statistic Value = 0.926, P-Value = 0.000) for the primary data collected from women employees in Chennai city. The statstic values of the both tests are the indication of normality in the data collected from the respondents.

FORMATION OF ORGANISATIONAL CAUSES OF STRESS (OCS) DOMINANT GROUPS

Cluster and Discriminant Analysis has been applied to identify the major groups of organisational causes of stress among the women employees in the Chennai city. The respondents have been classified into distinctive major groups significantly differentiated by 2 OCS Factors by applying quick cluster analysis and discriminant analysis. The results are shown in the table 6.

Table 6

Cluster and Discriminant Analysis - Organisational Causes of Stress Groups

Variables	Discriminant Coefficient (Function)		Discriminant Loadings (Funcion)		Group – 1 Mean (SD)	Group – 2 Mean (SD)	Group – 3 Mean (SD)	Tests of Equality of Group Means		
	1	2	1	2				Wilks' Lambda	F-Value	Sig.
Job Description Factor	0.768	-0.657	0.847	-0.532	29.103 (5.979)	61.626 (4.305)	45.751 (5.161)	0.129	2097.93	.000
Job Structure Factor	0.537	0.856	0.650	0.760	18.103 (4.082)	39.063 (3.085)	29.575 (5.452)	0.201	1235.74	.000

Wilks Lamba
(1 through 2 Wilks Lambda = 0.096; Chi-square = 1457.018, df = 4, Sig. = 0.000)
(2 Wilks Lambda = 0.995; Chi-square = 2.990, df = 1, Sig. = 0.084)

Eigen Value
Function 1: Eigen Value = 9.416 Variance 99.9% Canonical Correlation 0.951
Function 2: Eigen Value = 0.005 Variance 0.1% Canonical Correlation 0.069

Classification of Adopters Accuracy

		Organisational Causes of Stress Groups	Predicted Group Membership			Total
			Group – 1	Group – 2	Group – 3	
Original	Count	Group – 1	145	0	0	145
		Group – 2	0	286	0	286
		Group – 3	0	0	193	193
	%	Group – 1	100.0	0	0	100.0
		Group – 2	0	100.0	0	100.0
		Group – 3	0	0	100.0	100.0

Accuracy - 100.0% of Original – Validated Grouped Cases Correctly Classified

Organisational Causes of Stress Factors	Initial Cluster Centers			Final Cluster Centers		
	1	2	3	1	2	3
Job Description Factor	14.00	70.00	54.00	29.10	61.63	45.75
Job Structure Factor	25.00	45.00	10.00	18.10	39.06	29.58

Table 6 shows that three major groups have been formed significantly differentiated by both two OCS factors. The discriminant analysis has two discriminant functions, the most dominant discriminant function 1 with Eigen value of 9.416 and Canonical correlation of 0.951 and also with Wilk's Lambda value of 0.129 and the Chi-Sqaure value of 1457.018 at df 4 and 0.000 level of significance, explains

99.9% variance in the differentiation. In it, the most dominant differentiating factor is Job Description Factor and it has been named as Description Discriminant Function.

The Second most discriminant function 2 with Eigen Value of 0.005 and Canonical correlation of 0.069 and also with Wilk's Lambda value of 0.201 and Chi-Square value of 2.990 at 1 df and 0.000 level of significance, explains 0.01% of variance in differentiation. In it, the most dominating differentiating factor is Job Structure Factor. Therefore, it has been named as Structure Discriminant Function.

The table 6 shows that the first cluster formed has 145 respondents constituting of the 624 total respondents covered in the study. The second and the third clusters have 286 and 193 respondents comprising of 624 total respondents respectively. The table 6 reveals that 100.0 percentage of such classification is correct.

Thus, all 624 women employees have been classified into three major OCS groups of the Highest Organisational Stress Group, Moderate Organisational Stress Group and Low Organisational Stress Group significantly differentiated by both the two Organisational Causes of Stress Factors along with two discriminant functions of Description and Structure.

SIGNIFICANCE OF DIFFERENCE IN PERSONAL CHARACTERISTICS AND EMPLOYMENT CHARACTERISTICS OF THE RESPONDENTS WITH RESPECT TO ORGANISATIONAL CAUSES OF STRESS TOTAL SCORE AND FACTORS

Independent sample t-test and One-Way Analysis of Variance has been applied to identify the mean difference between the, Age, Educational Qualification, Monthly Income, Area of Living, Nature of family, Marital Status, Nature of Organisation, Schedule of Work, and Level of employment with regard to organisational causes of stress total score and factors. The results are tabulated and presented in tables from 7 to 15.

Table 7

Mean Differences Between Area of Living and Organisational Causes of Stress – Total Score & its Factors

Description	Area of Living	N	Mean	Std. Deviation	t-Value	P-Value	Mean Difference
Job Description Factor	Urban	345	50.075	13.650	1.834	0.067	2.050
	Semi – Urban	279	48.025	14.170			
Job Structure Factor	Urban	345	31.684	8.851	1.273	0.203	0.953
	Semi – Urban	279	30.731	9.816			
Organisational Causes of Stress – Total Score	Urban	345	81.759	21.665	1.667	0.096	3.003
	Semi – Urban	279	78.756	23.210			

Table 7 indicates that the area of living the respondents have a no mean significance difference between the dimensions of the organizational cause of stress (t-value = 1.667; P<0.096) with respect to the Job description (t-value = 1.834; p <0.067) and job structure (t-value = 1.273; p <0.953) at 5% level. Hence the empirical results proves that there is a no mean significance difference between organisational causes of stress total score and its factors with respect to area of living among urban area and semi urban of the respondents

Table 8

Mean Differences Between Nature of the Family and Organisational Causes of Stress – Total Score & its Factors

Description	Nature of the Family	N	Mean	Std. Deviation	t-Value	P-Value	Mean Difference
Job Description Factor	Nuclear Family	401	50.613	13.112	3.535	0.000**	4.071
	Joint Family	223	46.543	14.920			
Job Structure Factor	Nuclear Family	401	32.080	8.946	2.979	0.003**	2.300
	Joint Family	223	29.780	9.751			
Organisational Causes of Stress – Total Score	Nuclear Family	401	82.693	21.202	3.434	0.001**	6.370
	Joint Family	223	76.323	23.916			

Table 8 indicates that there is a significant mean difference between nature of the family groups and dimensions of organisational causes of stress total score (t- value = 3.434; P<0.001; Mean Difference = 6.370) with respect to its factor such as job description factor (t-value = 3.535; p <0.001; Mean Difference = 4.071) and job structure (t-value = 2.979; p <0.003; Mean Difference = 2.300) at 5% level. Hence the results proves that the respondents hailing from nuclear family group and joint family group have a significant mean difference with the organisational causes of stress total score and its factors such as job description and job structure of respondents.

Table 9

Mean Differences Between Marital Status and Organisational Causes of Stress – Total Score & its Factors

Description	Marital Status	N	Mean	Std. Deviation	t-Value	P-Value	Mean Difference
Job Description Factor	Married	405	49.686	13.123	1.289	0.198	1.504
	Unmarried	219	48.183	15.245			
Job Structure Factor	Married	405	31.723	8.926	1.703	0.089	1.326
	Unmarried	219	30.397	9.918			
Organisational Causes of Stress – Total Score	Married	405	81.410	21.186	1.508	0.132	2.830
	Unmarried	219	78.580	24.433			

Table 9 indicates that the marital status with respect to married and unmarried respondents has no significance mean difference between the dimension of the organizational cause of stress with respect to the Job description (t-value = 1.289; p <0.198) and job structure (t-value = 1.703; p <0.089) and total score of organisational causes of stress (t-value = 1.508; p<0.132) at 5% level.

Table 10

Mean Differences Between Nature of the Organisation and Organisational Causes of Stress – Total Score & its Factors

Description	Nature of the Organisation	N	Mean	Std. Deviation	t-Value	P-Value	Mean Difference
Job Description Factor	Private Sector	514	49.455	14.385	1.152	0.250	1.683
	Public Sector	110	47.773	11.395			
Job Structure Factor	Private Sector	514	31.385	9.612	0.738	0.461	0.722
	Public Sector	110	30.664	7.684			
Organisational Causes of Stress – Total Score	Private Sector	514	80.840	23.239	1.022	0.307	2.404
	Public Sector	110	78.436	17.932			

Table 10 indicates that the nature of the organization is working respondents with respect to private and public sector organisation has no significance mean difference between the dimension of the organizational cause of stress with respect to the Job description (t-value = 1.152; p <0.250) and job structure (t-value = 0.738; p <0.461) and total score of organisational causes of stress (t-value = 1.022; p<0.307) at 5% level.

Table 11

Mean Differences Between Age and Organisational Causes of Stress – Total Score & its Factors

Description	Age	N	Mean	Std. Deviation	F-Value (df: 3, 620)	P-Value
Job Description Factor	Between 20 to 30 Yrs	215	50.288	13.219	2.176	0.090
	Between 31 to 40 Yrs	256	47.598	14.606		
	Between 41 to 50 Yrs	97	49.320	13.634		
	Above 51 Yrs	56	51.679	13.253		
Job Structure Factor	Between 20 to 30 Yrs	215	31.749	8.838	0.837	0.474
	Between 31 to 40 Yrs	256	30.613	9.606		
	Between 41 to 50 Yrs	97	31.278	9.610		
	Above 51 Yrs	56	32.286	9.097		
Organisational Causes of Stress – Total Score	Between 20 to 30 Yrs	215	82.037	21.324	1.678	0.170
	Between 31 to 40 Yrs	256	78.211	23.455		
	Between 41 to 50 Yrs	97	80.598	22.346		
	Above 51 Yrs	56	83.964	21.136		

Table 11 indicates that age of the respondent has no significant difference between the dimensions of organisational causes of stress with respect to job description factor (F-Value = 2.176; P < 0.090), job structure factor (F-Value = 0.837; P<0.474) and total score of organisational causes of stress (F-Value = 1.678; P<0.170) at 5% level. The empirical result proves that the age group of above 51 years has higher stress cause with respect to the organizational cause of stress attributes.

Table 12

Mean Differences Between Educational Qualification and Organisational Causes of Stress – Total Score & its Factors

Description	Educational Qualification	N	Mean	Std. Deviation	F-Value (df: 4,619)	P-Value
Job Description Factor	School Level	76	50.895	13.002	1.996	0.094
	Graduate	167	47.263	13.288		
	Post – Graduate	248	50.444	14.404		
	Professional	110	48.655	13.977		
	Others	23	45.739	14.296		
Job Structure Factor	School Level	76	33.355	8.491	1.528	0.192
	Graduate	167	30.731	8.527		
	Post – Graduate	248	31.500	9.660		
	Professional	110	30.327	9.884		
	Others	23	30.000	9.954		
Organisational Causes of Stress – Total Score	School Level	76	84.250	20.824	1.704	0.147
	Graduate	167	77.994	20.970		
	Post – Graduate	248	81.944	23.439		
	Professional	110	78.982	22.602		
	Others	23	75.739	23.653		

Table 12 explores that the educational qualification of the respondents has no significant difference between the dimensions of organisational causes of stress with respect to job description factor (F-Value = 1.996; P<0.094) and job structure factor (F-Value = 1.528; P<0.192) and total score of organisational causes of stress (F-Value = 1.704; P<0.147) at 5% level. The result depicts that the school level respondents have a higher amount of stress when compare to the others.

Table 13

Differences Between Income and Organisational Causes of Stress – Total Score & its Factors

Description	Income	N	Mean	Std. Deviation	F-Value (df: 3,620)	P-Value
Job Description Factor	Below Rs. 20,000	156	50.718	12.723	1.827	0.141
	Rs.20,001 – Rs.40,000	312	49.346	14.189		
	Rs.40,001 – Rs.60,000	123	47.602	14.017		
	Above Rs.60,001	33	45.818	15.635		
Job Structure Factor	Below Rs. 20,000	156	32.333	8.723	2.519	0.057
	Rs.20,001 – Rs.40,000	312	31.516	9.291		
	Rs.40,001 – Rs.60,000	123	29.967	9.593		
	Above Rs.60,001	33	28.545	10.250		
Organisational Causes of Stress – Total Score	Below Rs. 20,000	156	83.051	20.626	2.239	0.083
	Rs.20,001 – Rs.40,000	312	80.862	22.773		
	Rs.40,001 – Rs.60,000	123	77.569	22.689		
	Above Rs.60,001	33	74.364	24.519		

Table 13 explores that the income level of the respondent has no significant difference between the dimensions of organisational causes of stress with respect to job description factor (F = 1.827; P<0.141) and job structure factor (F = 2.519; P<0.057) and total score of the organisational causes stress to the employees (F-Value = 2.239) at 5% level. The result depicts that the respondents with the income level below Rs.20,000 have a higher amount of stress when compare to the others.

Table 14

Mean Differences Between Job Nature and Organisational Causes of Stress – Total Score & its Factors

Description	Job Nature	N	Mean	Std. Deviation	F-Value (df: 2,621)	P-Value
Job Description Factor	Day Shift	319	48.912	13.475	6.028	0.003**
	Night Shift	133	46.323	15.145		
	Rotational Shift	172	51.808	13.299		
Job Structure Factor	Day Shift	319	31.069	8.852	10.116	0.000**
	Night Shift	133	28.789	10.239		
	Rotational Shift	172	33.517	8.861		
Organisational Causes of Stress – Total Score	Day Shift	319	79.981	21.447	8.099	0.000**
	Night Shift	133	75.113	24.647		
	Rotational Shift	172	85.326	21.386		

Table 14 indicates that there is a significant difference between nature of the job shift working and dimensions of organisational causes of stress with respect to job description factor (F-Value = 6.028; P<0.003) and job structure factor (F-Value = 10.116; P<0.000) and total score of organisational causes of stress (F-Value = 8.099; P<0.001) at 5% level. Furthermore the result depicts that the respondents with the rotational shift have a greater level of stress when compared with the other shifts.

Table 15

Differences Between Level of Employment and Organisational Causes of Stress – Total Score & its Factors

Description	Level of Employment	N	Mean	Std. Deviation	F-Value (df: 2,621)	P-Value
Job Description Factor	Low Level	188	49.080	13.834	4.785	0.009**
	Middle Level	294	50.616	13.902		
	Higher Level	142	46.246	13.662		
Job Structure Factor	Low Level	188	31.149	9.249	8.879	0.000**
	Middle Level	294	32.592	9.085		
	Higher Level	142	28.641	9.304		
Organisational Causes of Stress – Total Score	Low Level	188	80.229	22.170	6.736	0.001**
	Middle Level	294	83.207	22.289		
	Higher Level	142	74.887	22.043		

Table 15 explores that the level of the employment of the respondents with respect to low level, middle level and higher level employment have a significant difference in the job description factor (F-Value = 4.785; P<0.009), job structure factor (F-Value = 8.879; P<0.000) and total score of organisational causes of stress (F-Value = 6.736; P<0.001) at 5% level. The result depicts that the respondents in the middle level of the employment has a greater stress when compared to the other levels.

PERSONAL CAUSES OF STRESS:

The common causes of personal stress such as, loss of a job, financial burden, medical issues, depression, anxiety, anger, guilt and lower self-esteem which contributes to the enhancement in the stress level of the employees in commonly known as personal causes of stress. Exploratory factor analysis on eight personal causes of stress items was reduced into two predominated dimensions which accounted for 70.444% of the total variance with the total 5.636 Eigen value, 0.908 Kaiser-Meyer-Olkin Measure of Sampling Adequacy value (KMO) which indicate the meritorious level of prediction. Furthermore, the significance level of Bartlett's Test of Sphericity (BTS) was 0.000, which means that the data are appropriate for factor analysis. The results of the KMO and BTS tests show that the data meet the fundamental requirements of factor analysis. The overall cronbach's alpha co-efficient was 0.906 which is considered as acceptable level. The factor loadings ranged from 0.585 to 0.824 and the factors were labelled based on the items loaded. The results are presented below

Table 16

Exploratory Factor Analysis – Personal Causes of Stress

Particulars	Mean (SD)	Communalities	Variance (Eigen Value)	Reliability	Loadings
Work Life Imbalance Factor			36.644 (2.932)	0.867	
Lack of Concentration in Job (PCS1.4)	3.84 (1.184)	0.747			0.819
Not able to spend quality time with family (PCS1.3)	3.70 (1.212)	0.702			0.782
Not Spending time for own self development (PCS1.2)	3.80 (1.133)	0.713			0.776
Feeling of Inequality (PCS1.5)	3.71 (1.227)	0.694			0.742
Work Hindrance Factor			33.800 (2.704)	0.847	
Oragnisation does not provides Crèche facility (PCS1.6)	3.80 (1.208)	0.750			0.824
Inconvenience in Travelling to organisation (PCS1.8)	3.72 (1.243)	0.757			0.818
Lack of Time Management (PCS1.7)	3.84 (1.149)	0.729			0.769
Pressure to meet deadlines (PCS1.1)	3.75 (1.167)	0.544			0.585

Total Variance 70.444% ; Cronbach's Alpha Value = 0.906 (8 Items)

KMO and Bartlett's Test - Kaiser-Meyer-Olkin Measure of Sampling Adequacy. = 0.908

(Bartlett's Test of Sphericity Approx. Chi-Square = 2741.332; df = 28; Sig. = 0.000)

Work Life Imbalance Factor: Imbalance in the work life environment such as, work related issues, physical health problems due to work place atmosphere, emotional illness, lack of mental concentration in the work place, lack of joy and lack of contribution towards the achievement of organisational goals are commonly various inducers for the enhancement in the work life imbalance of the employees in an organisation. The factor loadings ranged from 0.742 to 0.819 with the variance of 36.644% and 2.932 of Eigen value. The items loaded under this dimension are Lack of Concentration in Job (PCS1.4), Not able to spend quality time with family (PCS1.3), Not Spending time for own self development (PCS1.2) and Feeling of Inequality (PCS1.5). Based on these items the factor named as "Work Life Imbalance Factor".

Work Hindrance Factor: There are two types of factors inducing the stress level of the employees, namely, hindrance and challenge. Hindrance stressors are stressful demands that are perceived as hindering progress toward personal attainment and accomplishment of goals and objectives of the organisation. The factor loadings ranged from 0.585 to 0.824 with the variance of 33.800% and 2.704 of Eigen value. The items loaded under this factor are Oragnisation does not provides Crèche facility (PCS1.6), Inconvenience in Travelling to organisation (PCS1.8), Lack of Time Management (PCS1.7) and Pressure to meet deadlines (PCS1.1). Based on this items it has been labeled as "Work Hindrance Factor".

Table 17

Descriptive Statistics – Personal Causes of Stress

Description	Mean	Std. Deviation	Skewness		Kurtosis	
			Statistic	Std. Error	Statistic	Std. Error
Work Life Imbalance Factor	15.0561	4.02461	-0.582	0.098	-0.411	0.195
Work Hindrance Factor	15.1170	3.94921	-0.489	0.098	-0.633	0.195
Personal Causes of Stress	**30.1731**	**7.39803**	**-0.580**	**0.098**	**-0.340**	**0.195**

The table 17 shows that out of maximum value of 20 *(5x4 **WLBF** variables)*, the mean value of 15.0561 is a robust measure of ***WLBF*** as the standard deviation is lower. The ***WLBF*** distribution has a slight negative skewness. Out of maximum value of 20 (*5x4 **WHF** variables),* the mean value of 15.1170 is a robust measure of **WHF** as the standard deviation is lower. The **WHF** distribution has a slight negative skewness. Out of maximum value of 40 (5*x8 PCS variables*), the mean value of 30.1731 is a robust measure of PCS as the standard deviation is lower. The PCS distribution has a slight negative skewness.

Table 18

Test of Normality – Personal Causes of Stress

Description	Kolmogorov-Smirnov[a]			Shapiro-Wilk		
	Statistic	Df	Sig.	Statistic	df	Sig.
Work Life Imbalance Factor	0.148	624	.000	0.919	624	.000
Work Hindrance Factor	0.127	624	.000	0.928	624	.000
Personal Causes of Stress	**0.141**	**624**	**.000**	**0.941**	**624**	**.000**

a. Lilliefors Significance Correction

Table 18 indicates that the by Kolmogorov-Smirnov Test of normality (Statistic Value = 0.141, P-Value = 0.000) and Shapiro-Wilk Test of Normality (Statistic Value = 0.941, P-Value = 0.000) for the primary data collected from women employees in Chennai city. The statstic values of the both tests are the indication of normality in the data collected from the respondents.

FORMATION OF PERSONAL CAUSES OF STRESS (PCS) DOMINANT GROUPS

Cluster and Discriminant Analysis has been applied to identify the major groups of personal causes of stress among the women employees in the Chennai city. The respondents have been classified into distinctive major groups significantly differentiated by 2 PCS Factors by applying quick cluster analysis and discriminant analysis. The results are shown in the table 19.

Table 19: Cluster and Discriminant Analysis - Personal Causes of Stress Groups

Variables	Discriminant Coefficient (Function)		Discriminant Loadings (Funcion)		Group – 1	Group – 2	Group – 3	Tests of Equality of Group Means		
	1	2	1	2	Mean (SD)	Mean (SD)	Mean (SD)	Wilks' Lambda	F-Value	Sig.
Work Life Imbalance Factor	0.644	0.765	0.765	-0.644	17.588 (2.384)	7.429 (1.949)	12.817 (2.027)	0.308	698.592	.000
Work Hindrance Factor	0.760	-0.650	0.650	0.760	17.843 (2.000)	8.079 (1.825)	12.329 (1.892)	0.201	967.748	.000

Wilks Lamba
(1 through 2 Wilks Lambda = 0.156; Chi-square = 1153.145, df = 4, Sig. = 0.000)
(2 Wilks Lambda = 0.984; Chi-square = 10.188, df = 1, Sig. = 0.001)

Eigen Value
Function 1: Eigen Value = 5.309 Variance 99.7% Canonical Correlation 0.917
Function 2: Eigen Value = 0.017 Variance 0.3% Canonical Correlation 0.128

Classification of Adopters Accuracy

		Personal Causes of Stress Groups	Predicted Group Membership			Total
			Group – 1	Group – 2	Group – 3	
Original	Count	Group – 1	362	0	2	364
		Group – 2	0	63	0	63
		Group – 3	0	6	191	197
	%	Group – 1	99.5	0	0.5	100.0
		Group – 2	0	100.0	0	100.0
		Group – 3	0	3.0	97.0	100.0

Accuracy – 98.7% of Original – Validated Grouped Cases Correctly Classified

Personal Causes of Stress Factors	Initial Cluster Centers			Final Cluster Centers		
	1	2	3	1	2	3
Work Life Imbalance Factor	12.00	4.00	17.00	17.59	7.43	12.82
Work Hindrance Factor	20.00	4.00	8.00	17.84	8.08	12.33

Table 19 shows that three major groups have been formed significantly differentiated by both two PCS factors. The discriminant analysis has two discriminant functions, the most dominant discriminant function 1 with Eigen value of 5.309 and Canonical correlation of 0.917 and also with Wilk's Lambda value of 0.156 and the Chi-Sqaure value of 1153.145 at df 4 and 0.000 level of significance, explains 99.7% variance in the differentiation. In it, the most dominant differentiating factor is Work Life Imbalance Factor and it has been named as Imbalance Discriminant Function.

The Second most discriminant function 2 with Eigen Value of 0.017 and Canonical correlation of 0.128 and also with Wilk's Lambda value of 0.984 and Chi-Square value of 10.188 at 1 df and 0.000 level of significance, explains 0.3% of variance in differentiation. In it, the most dominating differentiating factor is Work Hindrance Factor. Therefore, it has been named as Hindrance Discriminant Function.

The table 19 shows that the first cluster formed has 362 respondents constituting of the 624 total respondents covered in the study. The second and the third clusters have 63 and 191 respondents comprising of 624 total respondents respectively. The table 19 reveals that 98.7 percentage of such classification is correct.

Thus, all 624 women employees have been classified into three major OCS groups of the High Personal Stress Group, Moderate Personal Stress Group and Low Personal Stress Group significantly differentiated by both the two Personal Causes of Stress Factors along with two discriminant functions of Imbalance and Hindrance.

SIGNIFICANCE OF DIFFERENCE IN PERSONAL CHARACTERISTICS AND EMPLOYMENT CHARACTERISTICS OF THE RESPONDENTS WITH RESPECT TO PERSONAL CAUSES OF STRESS TOTAL SCORE AND FACTORS

Independent sample t-test and One-Way Analysis of Variance has been applied to identify the mean difference between the, Age, Educational Qualification, Monthly Income, Area of Living, Nature of family, Marital Status, Nature of Organisation, Schedule of Work, and Level of employment with regard to personal causes of stress total score and factors. The results are tabulated and presented in tables from 20 to 28.

Table 20

Differences Between Area of Living and Personal Causes of Stress – Total Score & its Factors

Description	Area of Living	N	Mean	Std. Deviation	t-Value	P-Value	Mean Difference
Work Life Imbalance Factor	Urban	345	15.148	4.050	0.633	0.527	0.205
	Semi - Urban	279	14.943	3.997			
Work Hindrance Factor	Urban	345	15.093	3.930	-0.170	0.865	-0.054
	Semi - Urban	279	15.147	3.980			
Personal Causes of Stress – Total Score	Urban	345	30.241	7.403	0.253	0.800	0.151
	Semi – Urban	279	30.090	7.404			

Table 20 indicates that the area of living of the respondents with respect to Urban area and semi urban area have a no significant mean difference between the dimensions of personal causes of stress such as work life imbalance factor (t-value = 0.633; p <0.527), work hindrance factor (t-value = -0.170; p <0.865) and total score of personal causes of stress (t-value = 0.253; p<0.800) at 5% level.

Table 21

Differences Between Nature of the Family and Personal Causes of Stress – Total Score & its Factors

Description	Nature of the Family	N	Mean	Std. Deviation	t-Value	P-Value	Mean Difference
Work Life Imbalance Factor	Nuclear Family	401	15.057	4.072	0.011	0.992	0.004
	Joint Family	223	15.054	3.947			
Work Hindrance Factor	Nuclear Family	401	15.152	4.057	0.298	0.766	0.098
	Joint Family	223	15.054	3.756			
Personal Causes of Stress – Total Score	Nuclear Family	401	30.209	7.492	0.165	0.869	0.102
	Joint Family	223	30.108	7.241			

Table 21 indicates that the nature of family type of the respondents with respect to nuclear family and joint family have no significant difference between the dimensions of personal causes of stress such as work life imbalance factor (t-value = 0.011; p <0.992) and work hindrance factor (t-value = 0.298; p <0.766) and total score of personal causes of stress (t-value = 0.165; p<0.869) at 5% level.

Table 22

Differences Between Marital Status and Personal Causes of Stress – Total Score & its Factors

Description	Marital Status	N	Mean	Std. Deviation	t-Value	P-Value	Mean Difference
Work Life Imbalance Factor	Married	405	15.146	4.193	0.756	0.450	0.255
	Unmarried	219	14.890	3.696			
Work Hindrance Factor	Married	405	15.138	3.939	0.183	0.855	0.061
	Unmarried	219	15.078	3.977			
Personal Causes of Stress – Total Score	Married	405	30.284	7.615	0.509	0.611	0.316
	Unmarried	219	29.968	6.992			

Table 22 explores that the marital status of the respondents group such as married and unmarried have no significant difference between the dimensions of personal causes of stress with respect to work life imbalance factor (t-value = 0.756; p <0.450) and work hindrance factor (t-value = 0.183; p <0.855) and total score of personal causes of stress (t-value = 0.509; p<0.611) at 5% level.

Table 23

Differences Between Nature of the Organisation and Personal Causes of Stress – Total Score & its Factors

Description	Nature of the Organisation	N	Mean	Std. Deviation	t-Value	P-Value	Mean Difference
Work Life Imbalance Factor	Private Sector	514	15.138	4.011	1.101	0.271	0.465
	Public Sector	110	14.673	4.082			
Work Hindrance Factor	Private Sector	514	15.218	3.981	1.381	0.168	0.572
	Public Sector	110	14.645	3.777			
Personal Causes of Stress – Total Score	Private Sector	514	30.356	7.442	1.336	0.182	1.038
	Public Sector	110	29.318	7.159			

Table 23 indicates that the nature of the organisation is respondents working such as private and public sector organisation have no significant mean difference between the dimensions of personal causes of stress with respect to work life imbalance factor (t-value = 1.101; p <0.271), work hindrance factor (t-value = 1.381; p <0.168) and total score of personal causes of stress (t-value = 1.336; p<0.182) at 5% level.

Table 24

Differences Between Age and Personal Causes of Stress – Total Score & its Factors

Description	Age	N	Mean	Std. Deviation	F-Value (df: 3, 620)	P-Value
Work Life Imbalance Factor	Between 20 to 30 Yrs	215	15.065	3.701	0.118	0.949
	Between 31 to 40 Yrs	256	15.129	4.034		
	Between 41 to 50 Yrs	97	15.000	4.474		
	Above 51 Yrs	56	14.786	4.438		
Work Hindrance Factor	Between 20 to 30 Yrs	215	15.423	3.773	0.706	0.549
	Between 31 to 40 Yrs	256	14.934	3.952		
	Between 41 to 50 Yrs	97	14.907	4.191		
	Above 51 Yrs	56	15.143	4.197		
Personal Causes of Stress – Total Score	Between 20 to 30 Yrs	215	30.488	6.755	0.211	0.889
	Between 31 to 40 Yrs	256	30.063	7.539		
	Between 41 to 50 Yrs	97	29.907	8.074		
	Above 51 Yrs	56	29.929	8.029		

Table 24 indicates that the age group of the respondents has no significant difference between the dimensions of personal causes of stress with respect to the work life imbalance factor (F-Value = 0.118; P<0.949) and work hindrance factor (F-Value = 0.706; P<0.549) and total score of personal causes of stress (F-Value = 0.211; P<0.889) at 5% level. The result proves that the age group between 20 to 30 years of respondents have a higher amount of personal stress when compare to the others age groups.

Table 25

Differences Between Educational Qualification and Personal Causes of Stress – Total Score & its Factors

Description	Educational Qualification	N	Mean	Std. Deviation	F-Value (df: 4,619)	P-Value
Work Life Imbalance Factor	School Level	76	16.211	3.803	**2.806**	**0.025****
	Graduate	167	14.635	4.308		
	Post - Graduate	248	15.270	3.782		
	Professional	110	14.536	4.070		
	Others	23	14.478	4.305		
Work Hindrance Factor	School Level	76	16.276	3.832	**3.531**	**0.007****
	Graduate	167	14.365	4.263		
	Post - Graduate	248	15.310	3.618		
	Professional	110	15.164	4.105		
	Others	23	14.435	3.764		
Personal Causes of Stress – Total Score	School Level	76	32.487	7.247	**3.428**	**0.009****
	Graduate	167	29.000	7.985		
	Post - Graduate	248	30.581	6.898		
	Professional	110	29.700	7.300		
	Others	23	28.913	7.609		

Table 25 explores that the educational qualification of the respondents such as school level, graduate, post graduate professionals and other educational qualification have a significant difference between the dimensions of personal causes of stress with respect to work life imbalance factor (F-Value = 2.806; P<0.025) and work hindrance factor (F-Value = 3.531; P<0.007) and total score of personal causes of stress (F- Value = 3.428; P<0.009) at 5% level. The result depicts that the school level respondents have a higher amount of personal stress when compare to the others.

Table 26

Differences Between Income and Personal Causes of Stress – Total Score & its Factors

Description	Income	N	Mean	Std. Deviation	F-Value (df: 3,620)	P-Value
Work Life Imbalance Factor	Below Rs. 20,000	156	15.468	3.533	3.454	0.016**
	Rs.20,001 – Rs.40,000	312	15.269	4.049		
	Rs.40,001 – Rs.60,000	123	14.382	4.479		
	Above Rs.60,001	33	13.606	3.724		
Work Hindrance Factor	Below Rs. 20,000	156	15.853	3.675	4.861	0.002**
	Rs.20,001 – Rs.40,000	312	15.215	3.986		
	Rs.40,001 – Rs.60,000	123	14.220	4.058		
	Above Rs.60,001	33	14.061	3.749		
Personal Causes of Stress – Total Score	Below Rs. 20,000	156	31.321	6.508	4.627	0.003**
	Rs.20,001 – Rs.40,000	312	30.484	7.492		
	Rs.40,001 – Rs.60,000	123	28.602	8.024		
	Above Rs.60,001	33	27.667	6.790		

Table 26 explores that the income level of the respondents has a significant difference between the dimensions of personal causes of stress with respect to work life imbalance factor (F-Value = 3.454; P<0.016) and work hindrance factor (F-Value = 4.861; P<0.002) with respect to the total score of personal cause of stress (F-Value = 4.627; P<0.003) at 5% level. The result depicts that the respondents with the income level below Rs.20,000 have a higher amount of personal stress when compare to the others.

Table 27

Differences Between Job Nature and Personal Causes of Stress – Total Score & its Factors

Description	Job Nature	N	Mean	Std. Deviation	F-Value (df: 2,621)	P-Value
Work Life Imbalance Factor	Day Shift	319	15.257	3.931	1.305	0.272
	Night Shift	133	14.586	4.092		
	Rotational Shift	172	15.047	4.135		
Work Hindrance Factor	Day Shift	319	15.097	3.778	3.602	0.028**
	Night Shift	133	14.451	4.226		
	Rotational Shift	172	15.669	3.981		
Personal Causes of Stress – Total Score	Day Shift	319	30.354	7.148	2.132	0.120
	Night Shift	133	29.038	7.880		
	Rotational Shift	172	30.715	7.423		

Table 27 indicates that the nature of the job of the respondents such as day shift, night shift and rotational shift working have a significant difference between the dimension of personal causes of stress with respect to the work hindrance factor (F = 3.602; P<0.028) at 5% level and the result depicts that the respondents with the rotational shift have a greater level of personal stress when compared with the other shifts. Furthermore, the working shift of the respondents there is no significant difference between the dimensions of personal causes of stress with respect to work life imbalance factor (F-Value = 1.305; P<0.272) and total score of personal cause of stress.

Table 28

Differences Between Level of Employment and Personal Causes of Stress – Total Score & its Factors

Description	Level of Employment	N	Mean	Std. Deviation	F-Value (df: 2,621)	P-Value
Work Life Imbalance Factor	Low Level	188	15.362	3.954	0.824	0.439
	Middle Level	294	14.966	4.083		
	Higher Level	142	14.838	3.999		
Work Hindrance Factor	Low Level	188	15.324	4.055	0.756	0.470
	Middle Level	294	15.143	3.927		
	Higher Level	142	14.789	3.859		
Personal Causes of Stress – Total Score	Low Level	188	30.686	7.501	0.850	0.428
	Middle Level	294	30.109	7.366		
	Higher Level	142	29.627	7.336		

Table 28 indicates that the employment level of the respondents has no significant difference between the dimensions of personal causes of stress with respect to work life imbalance factor (F-Value = 0.824; P<0.439) and work hindrance factor (F-Value = 0.756; P<0.470) and total score of personal causes of stress (F- Value = 0.850; P<0.428) at 5% level. The result depicts that the respondents in the low level of the employment has a greater personal stress when compared to the other levels.

IMPORTANCE REDUCE STRESS

Stress level can be mitigated by the application of various coping strategies in their day-to-day regular work practices or even in a personal time. Mitigation of stress level is very imperative in order to enhance the commitment and productivity of the employees with respect to the accomplishment of organisational objectives. Exploratory factor analysis on fifteen importance reduce stress items was reduced to two dimensions which accounted for 59.501% of the total variance with the total of 8.925 eigen values, 0.9333 Kaiser-Meyer-Olkin Measure of Sampling Adequacy value (KMO) which indicate the meritorious level of prediction. Furthermore, the significance level of Bartlett's Test of Sphericity (BTS) was 0.000, which means that the data are appropriate for factor analysis. The results of the KMO and BTS tests show that the data meet the fundamental requirements of factor analysis. The overall cronbach's alpha co-efficient was 0.934 which is considered as acceptable level. The factor loadings ranged from 0.527 to 0.851 and the factors were labelled based on the items loaded. The results are presented below.

Table 29

Exploratory Factor Analysis – Importance Reduce Stress

Particulars	Mean (SD)	Communalities	Variance (Eigen Value)	Reliability	Loadings
Job Enlargement Factor			37.172 (5.576)	0.916	
Flexible Work Timings (IRS1.12)	4.10 (0.840)	0.638			0.788
Providing Career Development Opportunities to Employees (IRS1.11)	4.14 (0.962)	0.617			0.770
Imparting Work-life Enrichment skills (IRS1.13)	4.11 (0.918)	0.626			0.756
Effective Time Management System (IRS1.15)	4.01 (0.987)	0.603			0.712
Involving Human Resource Practitioners for Effective Planning and Counseling (IRS1.14)	4.07 (0.835)	0.600			0.700
Adoptable Organisational Climate/Culture (IRS1.4)	4.00 (0.833)	0.542			0.668
Adopting Effective Motivational Methods (IRS1.9)	4.13 (0.878)	0.553			0.644
Proper Training and Development (IRS1.10)	4.13 (0.847)	0.538			0.622
Job Redesign (IRS1.6)	4.03 (0.887)	0.508			0.613
Providing Healthy and Safe Working Environment (IRS1.5)	4.17 (0.853)	0.571			0.597
Job Enrichment Factor			22.328 (3.349)	0.833	
Ensuring Job Security (IRS1.1)	4.31 (0.811)	0.731			0.851
Providing Fair and Good Salary/Compensation (IRS1.2)	4.18 (0.786)	0.628			0.744
Timely Reaction to Grievances (IRS1.7)	4.06 (0.958)	0.597			0.635
Employees' Participation in Decision-Making (IRS1.3)	4.06 (0.940)	0.620			0.595
Concern about Employee Health & Well-being (IRS1.8)	4.07 (0.868)	0.554			0.527

Total Variance 59.501% ; Cronbach's Alpha Value = 0.934 (15 Items)

KMO and Bartlett's Test - Kaiser-Meyer-Olkin Measure of Sampling Adequacy. = 0.933

(Bartlett's Test of Sphericity Approx. Chi-Square = 5450.399; df = 105; Sig. = 0.000)

Job Enlargement Factor: Job enlargement means increasing the scope of a job through extending the range of its job duties and responsibilities generally within the same level and periphery. Job enlargement involves combining various activities at the same level in the organization and adding them to the existing job. The factor loadings ranged from 0.597 to 0.788 with the variance of 37.172% and 5.576 of Eigen value. The items loaded under this factor are Flexible Work Timings (IRS1.12), Providing Career Development Opportunities to Employees (IRS1.11), Imparting Work-life Enrichment skills (IRS1.13), Effective Time Management System (IRS1.15), Involving Human Resource Practitioners for Effective Planning and Counseling (IRS1.14), Adoptable Organisational Climate/Culture (IRS1.4), Adopting Effective Motivational Methods (IRS1.9), Proper Training and Development (IRS1.10), Job Redesign (IRS1.6) and Providing Healthy and Safe Working Environment (IRS1.5). Based on this items it has been labeled as "Job Enlargement Factor".

Job Enrichment Factor: Job enrichment is a communal motivation method adopted by various organizations to give an employee extended and greater satisfaction in his work via enhanced commitment and performance. Job enrichment means allotting an employee additional duties and responsibilities that is previously assigned by his management or other higher-ranking positions. The factor loadings ranged from 0.527 to 0.851 with the variance of 22.328% and 3.349 of Eigen value. the items loaded under this factor are Ensuring Job Security (IRS1.1), Providing Fair and Good Salary/Compensation (IRS1.2), Timely Reaction to Grievances (IRS1.7), Employees' Participation in Decision-Making (IRS1.3) and Concern about Employee Health & Well-being (IRS1.8). Based on this items it has been labeled as "Job Enrichment Factor".

Table 30

Descriptive Statistics

Description	Mean	Std. Deviation	Skewness		Kurtosis	
			Statistic	Std. Error	Statistic	Std. Error
Job Enlargement Factor	40.8926	6.68073	-0.526	0.098	-0.648	0.195
Job Enrichment Factor	20.6731	3.38757	-0.793	0.098	-0.032	0.195
Importance Reduce Stress	61.5657	9.53706	-0.450	0.098	-0.841	0.195

The table 30 shows that out of maximum value of 75 *(5x15 **IRS** variables)*, the mean value of 61.5657 is a robust measure of **IRS** as the standard deviation is lower. The **IRS** distribution has a slight negative skewness. Out of maximum value of 50 (*5x10 JEF variables*), the mean value of **40.8926** is a robust measure of **JEF** as the standard deviation is lower. The **JEF** distribution has a slight negative skewness. Out of maximum value of 25 (5*x*5 *JENF variables*), the mean value of 20.6731 is a robust measure of **JENF** as the standard deviation is lower. The **JENF** distribution has a slight negative skewness.

Table 31

Test of Normality

Description	Kolmogorov-Smirnov[a]			Shapiro-Wilk		
	Statistic	Df	Sig.	Statistic	df	Sig.
Job Enlargement Factor	0.147	624	.000	0.934	624	.000
Job Enrichment Factor	0.138	624	.000	0.919	624	.000
Importance Reduce Stress	**0.123**	**624**	**.000**	**0.934**	**624**	**.000**

a. Lilliefors Significance Correction

Table 31 indicates that the by Kolmogorov-Smirnov Test of normality (Statistic Value = 0.123, P-Value = 0.000) and Shapiro-Wilk Test of Normality (Statistic Value = 0.934, P-Value = 0.000) for the primary data collected from women employees in Chennai city. The statstic values of the both tests are the indication of normality in the data collected from the respondents.

FORMATION OF IMPORTANCE TO REDUCE STRESS (IRS) DOMINANT GROUPS

Cluster and Discriminant Analysis has been applied to identify the major groups of importance to reduce stress among the women employees in the Chennai city. The respondents have been classified into distinctive major groups significantly differentiated by 2 importance to reduce stress factors by applying quick cluster analysis and discriminant analysis. The results are shown in the table 32.

Table 32

Cluster and Discriminant Analysis – Importance to Reduce Stress Groups

Variables	Discriminant Coefficient (Function)		Discriminant Loadings (Funcion)		Group – 1	Group – 2	Group – 3	Tests of Equality of Group Means		
	1	2	1	2	Mean (SD)	Mean (SD)	Mean (SD)	Wilks' Lambda	F-Value	Sig.
Job Enlargement Factor	0.903	-0.450	0.946	-0.323	39.679 (1.826)	46.769 (2.408)	30.463 (2.603)	0.116	2371.77	.000
Job Enrichment Factor	0.326	0.955	0.446	0.895	19.761 (2.404)	23.342 (1.335)	16.500 (2.658)	0.201	530.12	.000
Wilks Lamba										
(1 through 2 Wilks Lambda = 0.103; Chi-square = 1409.457, df = 4, Sig. = 0.000)										
(2 Wilks Lambda = 0.983; Chi-square = 10.649, df = 1, Sig. = 0.001)										
Eigen Value										
Function 1: Eigen Value =8.529 Variance 99.8% Canonical Correlation 0.946										
Function 2: Eigen Value = 0.017 Variance 0.2% Canonical Correlation 0.130										

Classification of Adopters Accuracy

		Importance Reduce Stress Groups	Predicted Group Membership			Total
			Group – 1	Group – 2	Group – 3	
Original	Count	Group – 1	209	0	0	209
		Group – 2	0	281	0	281
		Group – 3	0	0	193	193
	%	Group – 1	100.0	0	0	100.0
		Group – 2	0	100.0	0	100.0
		Group – 3	0	0	100.0	100.0

Accuracy - 100.0% of Original – Validated Grouped Cases Correctly Classified

Importance Reduce Stress Factor	Initial Cluster Centers			Final Cluster Centers		
	1	2	3	1	2	3
Job Enlargement Factor	40.00	50.00	27.00	39.68	46.77	30.46
Job Enrichment Factor	11.00	25.00	23.00	19.76	23.34	16.50

Table 32 shows that three major groups have been formed significantly differentiated by both two IRS factors. The discriminant analysis has two discriminant functions, the most dominant discriminant function 1 with Eigen value of 8.529 and Canonical correlation of 0.946 and also with Wilk's Lambda value of 0.103 and the Chi-Sqaure value of 1409.457 at df 4 and 0.000 level of significance, explains 99.8% variance in the differentiation. In it, the most dominant differentiating factor is Job Enlargement Factor and it has been named as Enlargement Discriminant Function.

The Second most discriminant function 2 with Eigen Value of 0.017 and Canonical correlation of 0.130 and also with Wilk's Lambda value of 0.983 and Chi-Square value of 10.649 at 1 df and 0.000 level of significance, explains 0.2% of variance in differentiation. In it, the most dominating differentiating factor is Job Enrichment Factor. Therefore, it has been named as Enrichment Discriminant Function.

The table 32 shows that the first cluster formed has 209 respondents constituting of the 624 total respondents covered in the study. The second and the third clusters have 281 and 193 respondents comprising of 624 total respondents respectively. The table 32 reveals that 98.7 percentage of such classification is correct.

Thus, all 624 women employees have been classified into three major IRS groups of the Highest Importance Group, Higher Importance Group and High Importance Group significantly differentiated by both the two Importance to Reduce Stress Factors along with two discriminant functions of Enlargement and Enrichment.

SIGNIFICANCE OF DIFFERENCE IN PERSONAL CHARACTERISTICS AND EMPLOYMENT CHARACTERISTICS OF THE RESPONDENTS WITH RESPECT TO IMPORTANCE TO REDUCE STRESS TOTAL SCORE AND FACTORS

Independent sample t-test and One-Way Analysis of Variance has been applied to identify the mean difference between the, Age, Educational Qualification, Monthly Income, Area of Living, Nature of family, Marital Status, Nature of Organisation, Schedule of Work, and Level of employment with regard to importance to reduce stress total score and factors. The results are tabulated and presented in tables from 33 to 41.

Table 33

Differences Between Area of Living and Importance Reduce Stress – Total Score & its Factors

Description	Area of Living	N	Mean	Std. Deviation	t-Value	P-Value	Mean Difference
Job Enlargement Factor	Urban	345	41.029	6.528	0.567	0.571	0.305
	Semi - Urban	279	40.724	6.873			
Job Enrichment Factor	Urban	345	20.887	3.214	1.757	0.079	0.478
	Semi - Urban	279	20.409	3.579			
Importance Reduce Stress – Total Score	Urban	345	61.916	9.200	1.020	0.308	0.783
	Semi - Urban	279	61.133	9.938			

Table 33 indicates that the area of living of the respondents in the urban and semi urban area has no significant mean difference between the dimensions of importance of reduce stress with respect to the job enlargement factor (t-value = 0.567; p <0.571) and job enrichment factor (t-value = 1.757; p <0.079) and total score of importance to reduce stress (t-value = 1.020; p<0.308) at 5% level.

Table 34

Differences Between Nature of the Family and Importance Reduce Stress – Total Score & its Factors

Description	Nature of the Family	N	Mean	Std. Deviation	t-Value	P-Value	Mean Difference
Job Enlargement Factor	Nuclear Family	401	41.080	6.473	0.938	0.348	0.524
	Joint Family	223	40.556	7.041			
Job Enrichment Factor	Nuclear Family	401	20.860	3.215	1.855	0.064	0.524
	Joint Family	223	20.336	3.661			
Importance Reduce Stress – Total Score	Nuclear Family	401	61.940	9.062	1.316	0.189	1.048
	Joint Family	223	60.892	10.323			

Table 34 indicates that the nature of family type of the respondents such as nuclear family and joint family group has no significant difference between the dimensions of importance to reduce stress with respect to the job enlargement factor (t-value = 0.938; p <0.524) and job enrichment factor (t-value = 1.855; p <0.064) and total score of importance to reduce stress (t-value = 1.316; p<0.189) at 5% level.

Table 35

Differences Between Marital Status and Importance Reduce Stress – Total Score & its Factors

Description	Marital Status	N	Mean	Std. Deviation	t-Value	P-Value	Mean Difference
Job Enlargement Factor	Married	405	41.099	6.635	1.048	0.295	0.587
	Unmarried	219	40.511	6.763			
Job Enrichment Factor	Married	405	20.748	3.361	0.753	0.452	0.214
	Unmarried	219	20.534	3.439			
Importance Reduce Stress – Total Score	Married	405	61.847	9.399	1.002	0.317	0.801
	Unmarried	219	61.046	9.787			

Table 35 explores that the marital status of the respondents such as married and unmarried respondents have no significant difference between the dimensions of importance to reduce stress with respect to job enlargement factor (t-value = 1.048; p <0.295) and work enrichment factor (t-value = 0.753; p <0.452) and total score of importance to reduce stress (t-value = 1.002; p<0.801) at 5% level.

Table 36

Differences Between Nature of the Organisation and Importance Reduce Stress – Total Score & its Factors

Description	Nature of the Organisation	N	Mean	Std. Deviation	t-Value	P-Value	Mean Difference
Job Enlargement Factor	Private Sector	514	41.161	6.638	2.180	0.030**	1.525
	Public Sector	110	39.636	6.766			
Job Enrichment Factor	Private Sector	514	20.757	3.413	1.336	0.182	0.475
	Public Sector	110	20.282	3.251			
Importance Reduce Stress – Total Score	Private Sector	514	61.918	9.524	2.001	0.046**	2.000
	Public Sector	110	59.918	9.466			

Table 36 explores that the nature of the organization working of the respondents private and public sector organisation have no significant difference between the dimensions of importance to reduce stress with respect to the job enlargement factor (t-value = 2.180; p <0.030) and total score of importance to reduce stress (t-value = 2.001; p<0.046) at 5% level. Furthermore, there is no significant difference between the job enrichment factor (t-value = 1.336; p <0.182) with the importance to reduce stress.

Table 37

Differences Between Age and Importance Reduce Stress – Total Score & its Factors

Description	Age	N	Mean	Std. Deviation	F-Value (df: 3, 620)	P-Value
Job Enlargement Factor	Between 20 to 30 Yrs	215	40.428	6.137	2.121	0.096
	Between 31 to 40 Yrs	256	40.606	7.081		
	Between 41 to 50 Yrs	97	41.763	6.645		
	Above 51 Yrs	56	42.482	6.658		
Job Enrichment Factor	Between 20 to 30 Yrs	215	20.554	3.242	1.438	0.231
	Between 31 to 40 Yrs	256	20.481	3.540		
	Between 41 to 50 Yrs	97	21.175	3.266		
	Above 51 Yrs	56	21.143	3.387		
Importance Reduce Stress – Total Score	Between 20 to 30 Yrs	215	60.981	8.843	2.035	0.108
	Between 31 to 40 Yrs	256	61.086	10.078		
	Between 41 to 50 Yrs	97	62.938	9.397		
	Above 51 Yrs	56	63.625	9.536		

Table 37 indicates that the age group of the respondents has no significant difference between the dimensions of importance to reduce stress with respect to job enlargement factor (F-Value = 2.121; P<0.096) and the job enrichment factor (F-Value = 1.438; P<0.231) and total score of importance reduce stress (F-Value = 2.035; P<0.108) at 5% level. The result depicts that the age group of above 51 years of respondents have a greater importance to reduce stress when compare to the others age groups.

Table 38

Differences Between Educational Qualification and Importance Reduce Stress – Total Score & its Factors

Description	Educational Qualification	N	Mean	Std. Deviation	F-Value (df: 4,619)	P-Value
Job Enlargement Factor	School Level	76	40.750	6.547	0.422	0.793
	Graduate	167	41.024	6.509		
	Post - Graduate	248	40.625	6.962		
	Professional	110	41.527	6.552		
	Others	23	40.261	6.144		
Job Enrichment Factor	School Level	76	20.816	2.775	0.821	0.512
	Graduate	167	20.772	3.460		
	Post - Graduate	248	20.512	3.536		
	Professional	110	20.973	3.090		
	Others	23	19.783	4.358		
Importance Reduce Stress – Total Score	School Level	76	61.566	8.871	0.558	0.693
	Graduate	167	61.796	9.514		
	Post - Graduate	248	61.137	9.917		
	Professional	110	62.500	9.115		
	Others	23	60.043	9.961		

Table 38 indicates that the educational qualification of the respondents has no significant difference between the dimensions of importance to reduce stress with respect to the job enlargement factor (F-Value = 0.422; P<0.793) and the job enrichment factor (F-Value = 0.821; P<0.512) and total score of the importance reduce stress (F-Value = 0.558; P<0.693) at 5% level. The result depicts that post graduate respondents have a higher importance to reduce stress when compare to the others.

Table 39

Differences Between Income and Importance Reduce Stress – Total Score & its Factors

Description	Income	N	Mean	Std. Deviation	F-Value (df: 3,620)	P-Value
Job Enlargement Factor	Below Rs. 20,000	156	40.564	6.654	0.484	0.694
	Rs.20,001 – Rs.40,000	312	40.849	6.694		
	Rs.40,001 – Rs.60,000	123	41.496	6.382		
	Above Rs.60,001	33	40.606	7.854		
Job Enrichment Factor	Below Rs. 20,000	156	20.538	3.336	0.355	0.785
	Rs.20,001 – Rs.40,000	312	20.641	3.482		
	Rs.40,001 – Rs.60,000	123	20.943	3.017		
	Above Rs.60,001	33	20.606	4.077		
Importance Reduce Stress – Total Score	Below Rs. 20,000	156	61.103	9.398	0.487	0.692
	Rs.20,001 – Rs.40,000	312	61.490	9.657		
	Rs.40,001 – Rs.60,000	123	62.439	8.867		
	Above Rs.60,001	33	61.212	11.518		

Table 39 explores that the income level of the respondents has no significant difference between the dimensions of importance reduce stress with respect to job enlargement factor (F-Value = 0.484; P<0.694) and the job enrichment factor (F- Value = 0.355; P<0.785) and total score of importance to reduce stress (F-Value = 0.487; P<0.692) at 5% level. The result depicts that the respondents income between Rs. 40,001 to RS.60,000 has greater importance to reduce stress when compared to the other income levels.

Table 40

Differences Between Job Nature and Importance Reduce Stress – Total Score & its Factors

Description	Job Nature	N	Mean	Std. Deviation	F-Value (df: 2,621)	P-Value
Job Enlargement Factor	Day Shift	319	41.006	6.542	4.508	0.011**
	Night Shift	133	39.489	7.395		
	Rotational Shift	172	41.767	6.204		
Job Enrichment Factor	Day Shift	319	20.884	3.238	7.359	0.001**
	Night Shift	133	19.692	3.941		
	Rotational Shift	172	21.041	3.058		
Importance Reduce Stress – Total Score	Day Shift	319	61.890	9.264	5.895	0.003**
	Night Shift	133	59.180	10.821		
	Rotational Shift	172	62.808	8.672		

Table 40 explores that the job nature of the respondents has significant difference between the dimensions of importance reduce stress with respect to job enlargement factor (F-Value = 4.508; P<0.011) and the job enrichment factor (F- Value = 7.359; P<0.001) and total score of the importance reduce stress (F-Value = 5.895; P<0.003) at 5% level. The result depicts that the respondents with the rotational shift has a high importance to reduce the stress when compared to the other shift respondents.

Table 41

Differences Between Level of Employment and Importance Reduce Stress – Total Score & its Factors

Description	Level of Employment	N	Mean	Std. Deviation	F-Value (df: 2,621)	P-Value
Job Enlargement Factor	Low Level	188	40.420	6.825	1.036	0.356
	Middle Level	294	41.286	6.430		
	Higher Level	142	40.704	6.989		
Job Enrichment Factor	Low Level	188	20.319	3.466	1.718	0.180
	Middle Level	294	20.905	3.227		
	Higher Level	142	20.662	3.585		
Importance Reduce Stress – Total Score	Low Level	188	60.739	9.705	1.369	0.255
	Middle Level	294	62.190	9.188		
	Higher Level	142	61.366	9.989		

Table 41 indicates that the employment level of the respondents has no significant difference between the dimensions of importance to reduce stress with respect to the job enlargement factor (F-Value = 1.036; P<0.356) and the job enrichment factor (F-Value = 1.718; P<0.180) and total score of the importance to reduce stress (F-Value = 1.369; P<0.255) at 5% level. The result depicts that the middle level employment group has greater importance to reduce the stress when compared to other levels.

QUALITY WORK LIFE

Quality of work life (QWL) is an extended and complex function to improve employee commitment in the work environment with seamless learning to adopt the organisational culture and change. QWL is a major determinant of job satisfaction, employee commitment and performance. QWL is mutually interrelated with the work environment and personal life of the employees where both are imperative in order to reduce the stress level of the employees. In a current dynamic business environment, every employee is maintenance of better QWL will facilitates the organisation to reduce the stress level among the employees. Exploratory factor analysis on twenty quality work life items was reduced to three factors which accounted for 67.400% of the total variance with the total of 13.479 Eigen values, 0.931 Kaiser-Meyer-Olkin Measure of Sampling Adequacy value (KMO) which indicate the meritorious level of prediction. Furthermore, the significance level of Bartlett's Test of Sphericity (BTS) was 0.000, which means that the data are appropriate for factor analysis. The results of the KMO and BTS tests show that the data meet the fundamental requirements of factor analysis. The overall cronbach's alpha co-efficient was 0.953 which is considered as acceptable level. The factor loadings ranged from 0.599 to 0.814 and the factors were labelled based on the items loaded. The results are presented below

Table 42

Exploratory Factor Analysis – Quality of Work Life

Particulars	Mean (SD)	Communalities	Variance (Eigen Value)	Reliability	Loadings
Organisational Culture Factor			33.236 (6.647)	0.943	
Management policies are flexible (QWL1.19)	4.04 (1.006)	0.723			0.780
Leaves offered is sufficient (QWL1.14)	4.07 (0.937)	0.657			0.773
Salary is fair and adequate (QWL1.17)	4.12 (0.888)	0.636			0.755
Career development opportunities are provided (QWL1.18)	4.05 (0.854)	0.668			0.735
Proper break / relaxing time is given (QWL1.11)	4.18 (0.909)	0.637			0.721
Transport facilities are comfortable and convenient (QWL1.15)	4.03 (0.968)	0.671			0.720
Resources are Adequate (QWL1.12)	4.11 (0.957)	0.651			0.708
Health, safety and welfare measures are followed effectively (QWL1.13)	4.21 (0.902)	0.659			0.703
Fringe benefits are good (QWL1.16)	4.11 (0.802)	0.571			0.683
Job recognition (QWL1.10)	4.18 (0.822)	0.605			0.636
Innovation and creativity is encouraged (QWL1.20)	3.99 (0.964)	0.558			0.607
Getting assistance from colleagues (QWL1.9)	4.25 (0.865)	0.601			0.599
Job Precision Factor			18.592 (3.718)	0.891	
Job clarity (QWL1.5)	4.18 (0.925)	0.774			0.744
Role clarity (QWL1.6)	4.18 (0.842)	0.763			0.740
Job rotation (QWL1.7)	4.21 (0.846)	0.704			0.726
Proper job design (QWL1.4)	4.15 (0.860)	0.768			0.648
Good and safe working environment is provided (QWL1.8)	4.23 (0.796)	0.606			0.625
Job Ontogenesis Factor			15.572 (3.114)	0.852	
Skills are matched with job (QWL1.1)	4.27 (0.931)	0.738			0.814
Challenging job (QWL1.2)	4.17 (0.844)	0.757			0.804
Work autonomy (QWL1.3)	4.17 (0.880)	0.736			0.721
Total Variance 67.400% ; Cronbach's Alpha Value = 0.953 (20 Items)					
KMO and Bartlett's Test - Kaiser-Meyer-Olkin Measure of Sampling Adequacy. = 0.931 (Bartlett's Test of Sphericity Approx. Chi-Square = 9733.096; df = 190; Sig. = 0.000)					

Organisational Culture Factor: Organisational Culture refers to an set of beliefs, values and policies that are followed by the every organisation in order to control and monitor the employees within the organisation. The organisational culture is very vital aspect which determines the commitment and interest of the employee to perform in an organisation effectively and efficiently. Organisational culture is the major dimension exhibit the maintenance of better QWL in the work premises. The factor loadings ranged from 0.599 to 0.780 with the variance of 33.236 % and 6.647 of Eigen value. The items loaded under this factor are Management policies are flexible (QWL1.19), Leaves offered is sufficient (QWL1.14), Salary is fair and adequate (QWL1.17), Career development opportunities are provided (QWL1.18), Proper break / relaxing time is given (QWL1.11), Transport facilities are comfortable and convenient (QWL1.15), Resources are Adequate (QWL1.12), Health, safety and welfare measures are followed effectively (QWL1.13), Fringe benefits are good (QWL1.16), Job recognition (QWL1.10), Innovation and creativity is encouraged (QWL1.20) and Getting assistance from colleagues (QWL1.9). Based on this items it has been labeled as "Organisational Culture Factor".

Job Precision Factor: Job assigned to every stakeholder in an organisation must be clearly indicated in an accurate way of measurement or operation with respect to their duties and responsibilities to finish their daily duties. Job carried by an employee must be accurately handling based on the requirement and demand of the employer to meet the expectations and organisational goals. The factor loadings ranged from 0.625 to 0.744 with the variance of 18.592% and 3.718 of Eigen value. The items loaded under this factor are Job clarity (QWL1.5), Role clarity (QWL1.6), Job rotation (QWL1.7), Proper job design (QWL1.4) and Good and safe working environment is provided (QWL1.8). Based on this items it has been labeled as "Job Precision Factor".

Job Ontogenesis Factor: The development of an individual potential and capabilities that induces the behavior towards the job in both the initial or maturity state of the work. The factor loadings ranged from 0.721 to 0.814 with the variance of 15.572% and 3.114 of Eigen value. The items loaded under this factor are Skills are matched with job (QWL1.1), Challenging job (QWL1.2) and Work autonomy (QWL1.3). Based on this items it has been labeled as "Job Ontogenesis Factor".

Table43

Descriptive Statistics

Description	Mean	Std. Deviation	Skewness		Kurtosis	
			Statistic	Std. Error	Statistic	Std. Error
Organisational Culture Factor	49.3285	8.52846	-0.774	0.098	-0.169	0.195
Job Precision Factor	20.9551	3.56745	-1.210	0.098	1.500	0.195
Job Ontogenesis Factor	13.7423	1.61550	-1.216	0.098	1.320	0.195
Quality Work Life	**82.8974**	**12.98075**	**-0.683**	**0.098**	**-0.366**	**0.195**

The table 43 shows that out of maximum value of 100 *(5x20 QWL variables)*, the mean value of 82.8974 is a robust measure of **QWL** as the standard deviation is lower. The **QWL** distribution has a slight negative skewness. Out of maximum value of 60 *(5x12 OCF variables)*, the mean value of **49.3285** is a robust measure of **OCF** as the standard deviation is lower. The **OCF** distribution has a slight negative skewness. Out of maximum value of 25 (*5x5 JENF variables*), the mean value of 20.9551 is a robust measure of **JPF** as the standard deviation is lower. The **JPF** distribution has a slight negative skewness. Out of maximum value of 15 (*5x3 JOF variables*), the mean value of 13.7423 is a robust measure of **JOF** as the standard deviation is lower. The **JOF** distribution has a slight negative skewness.

Table 44

Test of Normality

Description	Kolmogorov-Smirnov[a]			Shapiro-Wilk		
	Statistic	Df	Sig.	Statistic	df	Sig.
Organisational Culture Factor	0.152	624	.000	0.919	624	.000
Job Precision Factor	0.168	624	.000	0.885	624	.000
Job Ontogenesis Factor	0.228	624	.000	0.846	624	.000
Quality Work Life	0.158	624	.000	0.930	624	.000

a. Lillefors Significance Correction

Table 44 indicates that the by Kolmogorov-Smirnov Test of normality (Statistic Value = 0.158, P-Value = 0.000) and Shapiro-Wilk Test of Normality (Statistic Value = 0.930, P-Value = 0.000) for the primary data collected from women employees in Chennai city. The statstic values of the both tests are the indication of normality in the data collected from the respondents.

FORMATION OF QUALITY OF WORK LIFE (QWL) DOMINANT GROUPS

Cluster and Discriminant Analysis has been applied to identify the major groups of quality of work life among the women employees in the Chennai city. The respondents have been classified into distinctive major groups significantly differentiated by quality of work life factors by applying quick cluster analysis and discriminant analysis. The results are shown in the table 45.

Table 45

Cluster and Discriminant Analysis - Quality Work Life Groups

Variables	Discriminant Coefficient (Function)		Discriminant Loadings (Funcion)		Group – 1 Mean (SD)	Group – 2 Mean (SD)	Group – 3 Mean (SD)	Tests of Equality of Group Means		
	1	2	1	2				Wilks' Lambda	F-Value	Sig.
Organisational Culture Factor	0.885	0.193	0.920	0.239	55.699 (2.925)	34.573 (4.490)	45.173 (3.651)	0.161	1618.46	0.000
Job Precision Factor	0.400	-0.828	0.247	0.615	23.017 (1.946)	15.333 (3.678)	20.048 (1.954)	0.414	439.20	0.000
Job Ontogenesis Factor	-0.022	0.882	0.477	-0.496	14.504 (1.045)	12.425 (1.888)	13.013 (1.563)	0.715	123.95	0.000

Wilks Lamba
(1 through 2 Wilks Lambda = 0.131; Chi-square = 1259.84, df = 6, Sig. = 0.000)
(2 Wilks Lambda = 0.937; Chi-square = 40.293, df = 2, Sig. = 0.000)

Eigen Value
Function 1: Eigen Value = 6.149 Variance 98.9% Canonical Correlation 0.927
Function 2: Eigen Value = 0.067 Variance 1.1% Canonical Correlation 0.251

Classification of Adopters Accuracy

		Quality Work Life Groups	Predicted Group Membership			Total
			Group – 1	Group – 2	Group – 3	
Original	Count	Group – 1	337	0	6	343
		Group – 2	0	90	6	96
		Group – 3	2	2	181	185
	%	Group – 1	98.3	0	1.7	100.0
		Group – 2	0	93.8	6.3	100.0
		Group – 3	1.1	1.1	97.8	100.0

Accuracy – 97.4% of Original – Validated Grouped Cases Correctly Classified

Quality of Work Life Factors	Initial Cluster Centers			Final Cluster Centers		
	1	2	3	1	2	3
Organisational Culture Factor	60.00	23.00	43.00	55.70	34.57	45.17
Job Precision Factor	25.00	18.00	10.00	23.02	15.33	20.05
Job Ontogenesis Factor	15.30	14.30	9.30	14.50	12.42	13.01

Table 45 shows that three major groups have been formed significantly differentiated by both two QWL factors. The discriminant analysis has two discriminant functions, the most dominant discriminant function 1 with Eigen value of 6.149 and Canonical correlation of 0.927 and also with Wilk's Lambda value of 0.131 and the Chi-Sqaure value of 1259.84 at df 6 and 0.000 level of significance, explains 98.9% variance in the differentiation. In it, the most dominant differentiating factor is Oraganisational Culture Factor followed by Job Precision Factor and it has been named as Culture Discriminant Function.

The Second most discriminant function 2 with Eigen Value of 0.067 and Canonical correlation of 0.251 and also with Wilk's Lambda value of 0.937 and Chi-Square value of 40.293 at 2 df and 0.000 level of significance, explains 1.1% of variance in differentiation. In it, the most dominating differentiating factor is Job Ontogenesis Factor. Therefore, it has been named as Ontogenesis Discriminant Function.

The table 45 shows that the first cluster formed has 337 respondents constituting of the 624 total respondents covered in the study. The second and the third clusters have 90 and 181 respondents comprising of 624 total respondents respectively. The table 45 reveals that 97.4 percentage of such classification is correct.

Thus, all 624 women employees have been classified into three major QWL groups of the Highest Work Life Group, Higher Work Life Group and High Work Life Group significantly differentiated by all the three Quality Work of Life Factors along with two discriminant functions of Culture and Ontogenesis.

SIGNIFICANCE OF DIFFERENCE IN PERSONAL CHARACTERISTICS AND EMPLOYMENT CHARACTERISTICS OF THE RESPONDENTS WITH RESPECT QUALITY OF WORK LIFE TOTAL SCORE AND FACTORS

Independent sample t-test and One-Way Analysis of Variance has been applied to identify the mean difference between the, Age, Educational Qualification, Monthly Income, Area of Living, Nature of family, Marital Status, Nature of Organisation, Schedule of Work, and Level of employment with regard to quality of work life total score and factors. The results are tabulated and presented in tables from 46 to 54.

Table 46

Differences Between Area of Living and Quality Work Life – Total Score & its Factors

Description	Area of Living	N	Mean	Std. Deviation	t-Value	P-Value	Mean Difference
Organisational Culture Factor	Urban	345	48.933	8.869	-1.288	0.198	-0.884
	Semi – Urban	279	49.817	8.076			
Job Precision Factor	Urban	345	20.849	3.525	-0.824	0.410	-0.237
	Semi – Urban	279	21.086	3.621			
Job Ontogenesis Factor	Urban	345	13.662	1.667	-1.376	0.169	-0.179
	Semi – Urban	279	13.841	1.547			
Quality Work Life – Total Score	Urban	345	82.287	13.240	-1.307	0.192	-1.365
	Semi – Urban	279	83.652	12.635			

Table 46 indicates that the area of living of the respondents has no significant mean difference between dimensions of quality work life with respect to the organizational culture factor (t-value = -1.288; p <0.198), job precision factor (t-value = -0.824; p <0.410) and job ontogenesis factor (t-value = - 1.376; p <0.169) and total score of quality work life (t-value = -1.307; p<0.192) at 5% level.

Table 47

Differences Between Nature of the Family and Quality Work Life – Total Score & its Factors

Description	Nature of the Family	N	Mean	Std. Deviation	t-Value	P-Value	Mean Difference
Organisational Culture Factor	Nuclear Family	401	48.696	8.782	-2.496	0.013**	-1.771
	Joint Family	223	50.466	7.946			
Job Precision Factor	Nuclear Family	401	20.736	3.587	-2.066	0.039**	-0.614
	Joint Family	223	21.350	3.506			
Job Ontogenesis Factor	Nuclear Family	401	13.664	1.653	-1.624	0.105	-0.219
	Joint Family	223	13.883	1.540			
Quality Work Life – Total Score	Nuclear Family	401	81.895	13.271	-2.598	0.010**	-2.804
	Joint Family	223	84.700	12.266			

Table 47 indicates that the nature of family type of the respondents such as nuclear family and joint family groups have a significant mean difference between the dimensions of quality of work life with respect to organizational culture factor (t- value = -2.496; p <0.013) and job precision factor (t-value = -2.066; p <0.039) and total score of the quality of work life (t-value = -2.598; p<0.010) at 5% level. The result proves that the join family of the respondents has higher perception of stress with respect to quality of work life dimensions and its total score. Furthermore, there is no significant difference between the job ontogenesis factor (t-value = - 1.624; p <0.105) with respect to the dimension of quality work life.

Table 48

Differences Between Marital Status and Quality Work Life – Total Score & its Factors

Description	Marital Status	N	Mean	Std. Deviation	t-Value	P-Value	Mean Difference
Organisational Culture Factor	Married	405	49.158	8.568	-0.679	0.497	-0.486
	Unmarried	219	49.644	8.465			
Job Precision Factor	Married	405	20.857	3.653	-0.936	0.349	-0.280
	Unmarried	219	21.137	3.404			
Job Ontogenesis Factor	Married	405	13.715	1.637	-0.578	0.564	-0.078
	Unmarried	219	13.793	1.578			
Quality Work Life – Total Score	Married	405	82.585	13.135	-0.817	0.414	-0.890
	Unmarried	219	83.475	12.699			

Table 48 indicates that the marital status of the respondents has no significant difference between the dimensions of quality of work life with respect to organizational culture factor (t-value = -0.679; p <0.497), job precision factor (t-value = -0.936; p <0.349) and job ontogenesis factor (t-value = - 0.578; p <0.564) and total score of the quality work life (t-value = -0.817; p<0.414) at 5% level.

Table 49

Differences Between Nature of the Organisation and Quality Work Life – Total Score & its Factors

Description	Nature of the Organisation	N	Mean	Std. Deviation	t-Value	P-Value	Mean Difference
Organisational Culture Factor	Private Sector	514	49.840	8.443	3.266	0.001**	2.904
	Public Sector	110	46.936	8.556			
Job Precision Factor	Private Sector	514	21.119	3.502	2.486	0.013**	0.928
	Public Sector	110	20.191	3.784			
Job Ontogenesis Factor	Private Sector	514	13.847	1.549	3.521	0.000**	0.592
	Public Sector	110	13.255	1.824			
Quality Work Life – Total Score	Private Sector	514	83.722	12.788	3.459	0.001**	4.676
	Public Sector	110	79.045	13.238			

Table 49 explores that the nature of the organization such as private and public sector organisation respondents working has significant difference between the dimensions of quality work life with respect to organizational culture factor (t-value = 3.266; p <0.001), job precision factor (t-value = 2.486; p <0.013) and job ontogenesis factor (t-value =3.521; p <0.000) and total score of the quality work life (t-value = 3.459; p<0.001) at 5% level.

Table 50

Differences Between Age and Quality Work Life – Total Score & its Factors

Description	Age	N	Mean	Std. Deviation	F-Value (df: 3, 620)	P-Value
Organisational Culture Factor	Between 20 to 30 Yrs	215	48.223	8.311	2.679	0.046**
	Between 31 to 40 Yrs	256	50.152	8.851		
	Between 41 to 50 Yrs	97	50.227	8.200		
	Above 51 Yrs	56	48.250	7.998		
Job Precision Factor	Between 20 to 30 Yrs	215	20.679	3.234	1.004	0.391
	Between 31 to 40 Yrs	256	21.219	3.743		
	Between 41 to 50 Yrs	97	20.784	3.964		
	Above 51 Yrs	56	21.107	3.223		
Job Ontogenesis Factor	Between 20 to 30 Yrs	215	13.551	1.647	1.706	0.165
	Between 31 to 40 Yrs	256	13.878	1.590		
	Between 41 to 50 Yrs	97	13.826	1.555		
	Above 51 Yrs	56	13.711	1.682		
Quality Work Life – Total Score	Between 20 to 30 Yrs	215	81.223	12.479	2.268	0.079
	Between 31 to 40 Yrs	256	84.172	13.427		
	Between 41 to 50 Yrs	97	83.773	13.152		
	Above 51 Yrs	56	81.982	12.008		

Table 50 indicates that the age group of the respondents has significant difference between dimensions of quality work life with respect to organizational culture factor (F-Value = 2.679; P<0.046) at 5% level and the result depicts that the age group between 31 to 40 years of respondents have a greater quality work life when compare to the others age groups. Furthermore, the tables shows that there is no significant difference between the job precision factor(F = 1.004; P > 0.391) and job ontogenesis factor(F = 1.706; P>0.165) and total score of quality work life dimension (F-Value = 2.268; P>0.079).

Table 51

Differences Between Educational Qualification and Quality Work Life – Total Score & its Factors

Description	Educational Qualification	N	Mean	Std. Deviation	F-Value (df: 4,619)	P-Value
Organisational Culture Factor	School Level	76	49.013	8.193	1.428	0.223
	Graduate	167	48.305	8.116		
	Post - Graduate	248	50.109	8.564		
	Professional	110	48.982	9.241		
	Others	23	51.043	8.276		
Job Precision Factor	School Level	76	20.211	3.865	4.379	0.002**
	Graduate	167	20.275	3.714		
	Post - Graduate	248	21.556	3.130		
	Professional	110	21.209	3.648		
	Others	23	20.652	4.427		
Job Ontogenesis Factor	School Level	76	13.208	2.001	4.693	0.001**
	Graduate	167	13.563	1.733		
	Post - Graduate	248	13.994	1.348		
	Professional	110	13.718	1.628		
	Others	23	14.213	1.379		
Quality Work Life – Total Score	School Level	76	81.132	13.553	2.593	0.036**
	Graduate	167	80.904	13.005		
	Post - Graduate	248	84.629	12.117		
	Professional	110	82.836	13.895		
	Others	23	84.826	13.627		

Table 51 indicates that the educational qualification of the respondents has significant difference between the dimensions of quality work life with respect to job precision factor (F-Value = 4.379; P<0.002) and job ontogenesis factor (F-Value = 4.693; P<0.001) and total score of the quality work life (F-Value = 2.593; p<0.036) at 5% level. The results depicts that the others has a greater quality work life when compared to the other qualification of the respondents. Furthermore, the tables shows that there is no significant difference between the dimension of quality of work life with respect to organizational culture factor (F =1.428; P>0.223).

Table 52

Differences Between Income and Quality Work Life – Total Score & its Factors

Description	Income	N	Mean	Std. Deviation	F-Value (df: 3,620)	P-Value
Organisational Culture Factor	Below Rs. 20,000	156	48.269	8.529	1.794	0.147
	Rs.20,001 – Rs.40,000	312	49.625	8.411		
	Rs.40,001 – Rs.60,000	123	50.309	8.209		
	Above Rs.60,001	33	47.879	10.349		
Job Precision Factor	Below Rs. 20,000	156	20.462	3.427	1.703	0.165
	Rs.20,001 – Rs.40,000	312	21.061	3.536		
	Rs.40,001 – Rs.60,000	123	21.374	3.540		
	Above Rs.60,001	33	20.727	4.425		
Job Ontogenesis Factor	Below Rs. 20,000	156	13.524	1.617	1.319	0.267
	Rs.20,001 – Rs.40,000	312	13.794	1.590		
	Rs.40,001 – Rs.60,000	123	13.861	1.670		
	Above Rs.60,001	33	13.845	1.622		
Quality Work Life – Total Score	Below Rs. 20,000	156	81.013	12.777	2.002	0.112
	Rs.20,001 – Rs.40,000	312	83.404	12.801		
	Rs.40,001 – Rs.60,000	123	84.431	12.697		
	Above Rs.60,001	33	81.303	15.840		

Table 52 explores that the income level of the respondents has no significant difference between the dimensions of quality work life with respect to the organizational culture factor (F-Value = 1.794; P<0.147), job precision factor (F-Value = 1.703; P<0.165) and job ontogenesis factor (F-Value = 1.319; P<0.267) and total score of the quality work life (F-Value = 2.002; p<0.112) at 5% level and the results depicts that the respondents with the income level of Rs.40,001 to Rs.60,000 has a greater quality of life when compared to other income groups.

Table 53

Differences Between Job Nature and Quality Work Life – Total Score & its Factors

Description	Job Nature	N	Mean	Std. Deviation	F-Value (df: 2,621)	P-Value
Organisational Culture Factor	Day Shift	319	48.527	8.477	6.183	0.002**
	Night Shift	133	51.571	8.189		
	Rotational Shift	172	49.081	8.626		
Job Precision Factor	Day Shift	319	20.655	3.689	4.660	0.010**
	Night Shift	133	21.767	3.364		
	Rotational Shift	172	20.884	3.411		
Job Ontogenesis Factor	Day Shift	319	13.588	1.699	3.802	0.023**
	Night Shift	133	14.037	1.571		
	Rotational Shift	172	13.800	1.457		
Quality Work Life – Total Score	Day Shift	319	81.542	12.971	6.671	0.001**
	Night Shift	133	86.383	12.614		
	Rotational Shift	172	82.715	12.857		

Table 53 explores that the nature of the job of the respondents shift wise working has significant difference between the dimensions of quality work life with respect to the organizational culture factor (F-Value = 6.183; P<0.002), job precision factor (F-Value = 4.660; P<0.010) and job ontogenesis factor (F-Value = 3.802; P<0.023) and total score of quality work life (F-Value = 6.671; P<0.001) at 5% level. The results depicts that the respondents with the day shift has the greater quality of life when compared to the other shifts.

Table 54

Differences Between Level of Employment and Quality Work Life – Total Score & its Factors

Description	Level of Employment	N	Mean	Std. Deviation	F-Value (df: 2,621)	P-Value
Organisational Culture Factor	Low Level	188	47.936	9.213	3.721	0.025**
	Middle Level	294	50.058	7.920		
	Higher Level	142	49.662	8.640		
Job Precision Factor	Low Level	188	20.436	3.583	2.876	0.057
	Middle Level	294	21.197	3.495		
	Higher Level	142	21.141	3.649		
Job Ontogenesis Factor	Low Level	188	13.534	1.605	2.667	0.070
	Middle Level	294	13.783	1.654		
	Higher Level	142	13.934	1.527		
Quality Work Life – Total Score	Low Level	188	80.681	13.653	3.972	0.019**
	Middle Level	294	83.918	12.570		
	Higher Level	142	83.718	12.631		

Table 54 indicates that the employment level of the respondents has significant difference between the dimensions of quality work life with respect to organizational culture factor (F-Value = 3.721; P<0.025) and total score of quality work life (F-Value = 3.972; P<0.019) at 5% level and the result depicts that the middle level of respondents have a greater quality work life when compare to the others levels. Furthermore, the tables shows that there is no significant difference between the job precision factor (F-Value = 2.876; P<0.057) and job ontogenesis factor (F-Value = 2.667; P <0.070) with respect to the quality work life dimensions.

STRUCTURAL EQUATION MODEL ON DETERMINANTS OF QUALITY OF WORK LIFE OF WOMEN EMPLOYEES

Model has been developed to test the structural influence of organisational causes of stress, personal causes of stress and importance to reduce stress on quality of work life of women employees. Structural Equation Modeling (SEM) has used to bring out the casual relationships using combination of stress factors. Unlike other methods SEM does not have limitation in number of variables adopted as it is considered to be one of the best approaches in eliminating errors from the variables. There is no difficulty in hypothesis testing as SEM only adopts confirmatory approaches rather than the exploratory approaches. There would be many sub-Criteria considered to be tested which brought out the very decision making by people participation in the survey.

The relative weight age arrive from SEM is considered highly reliable then through to any other approaches this model also takes measurement error into account when analysing the data statistically. SEM is capable of estimating or assessing measurement error. It can incorporate both observed and latent variables and require less reliance on basic statistical method.

Table 55

Structural Equation Modeling – Determinants of Quality of Work Life

Path	Std Estimate	C.R.	P	Label
Job Enrichment Influenced by Wok Life Imbalance Factor	0.191	5.538	***	Significant
Job Enlargement Influenced by Job Structure Factor	0.111	2.233	0.026	Significant
Job Enlargement Influenced by Job Description Factor	0.099	1.999	0.045	Significant
Job Enrichment Influenced by Work Hindrance Factor	0.100	2.240	0.023	Significant
Quality of Work Life Influenced by Job Enlargement	0.235	4.072	***	Significant
Quality of Work Life Influenced by Job Enrichment	0.130	2.249	0.024	Significant
Quality of Work Life Influenced by Job Description Factor	-0.116	-1.607	0.108	Not Significant
Quality of Work Life Influenced by Job Structure Factor	0.128	1.989	0.049	Significant
Quality of Work Life Influenced by Work Life Imbalance Factor	0.318	4.340	***	Significant
Quality of Work Life Influenced by Work Hindrance Factor	0.105	2.056	0.044	Significant
Model Fit				

Model Fit	CMIN/df: 5.321/4 = 1.330, GFI: 0.998, AGFI: 0.998, RMSEA:0.023, NFI: 0.997, TLI: 0.997, CFI: 0.999, SRMR: 0.0197

Figure 1

Determinants of Quality of Work Life

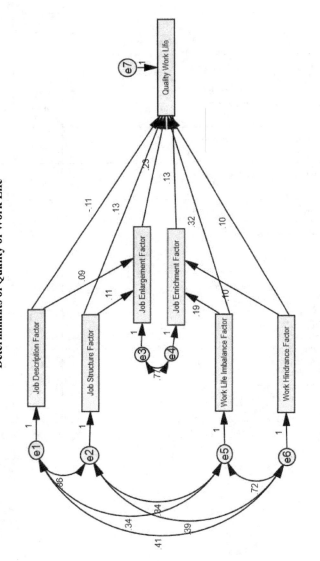

Table - 56

Criteria for Structural Equation Model Analysis

Sl. No.	Test Factor	Value	Suggested Value
1.	Chi-square Value	5.321	Range from as high as 5.0 (Wheaton et al 1977) to as low as 2.0 (Tabachnic et al 2007)
2.	P Value	0.090	> 0.5 (Hair et al 1998)
3.	GFI	0.998	> 0.90 (Hair et al 2006)
4.	AGFI	0.998	>0.90 (Daire et al. 2008)
5.	CFI	0.999	> 0.90 (Hu and Bentler, 1999)
6.	RMR	0.019	< 0.08 (Hair et al 2006)
7.	RMSEA	0.023	<0.08 (Hair et al 2006)
8.	NFI	0.997	>0.95 (Bentler et al 1980)

The table 55 and 56, it is found that the calculated P value is 0.090 which is greater than 0.05 representing perfect fitness. GFI (Goodness of Fit Index) value and AGFI (Adjusted Goodness of Fit Index) values are greater than 0.9 which implies a good fit model. The calculated CFI (Comparative Fit Index) Value is 0.999 indicating a good fit and also found that RMR (Root Mean Square Residuals) value 0.019 and RMSEA (Root Mean Square Error of Approximation) value is 0.023 shows a perfect fit of model. The structural equation model indicates that it has goodness-of-fit and it clearly explores that organisational causes of stress have significant and negative influence on quality of work life whereas, personal causes of stress and importance to reduce stress have significant and positive prediction for the inducement in the quality of work life of women employees. Except Job Description factor all the other stress factors have significant relationship with the quality of work life. Higher is the organisational causes of stress lesser is the quality of work life and higher is the personal causes of stress and importance to reduce stress higher is the quality of work life among women employees.

INFLUENCE OF STRESS ON QUALITY OF WORK LIFE OF WOMEN EMPLOYEES

The Multiple Regression Analysis has been applied to study the significance of influence of influence of organisational causes of stress factors, personal causes of stress, importance to reduce stress on total quality of work life and the results are shown in Table 57.

Table - 57

Significant Predictor of Quality of Work Life

Significant Predictors	Standardized Coefficients Beta	t - value	P - Value
(Constant)		15.468	.000**
Job Description Factor	-0.117	-1.596	0.111
Job Structure Factor	0.124	1.975	0.049
Work Life Imbalance Factor	0.285	.338	0.736
Work Hindrance Factor	.105	1.994	0.044
Job Enlargement Factor	.236	4.050	0.000
Job Enrichment Factor	.130	2.236	0.026
a. Dependent Variable: Quality Work Life			

Model Summary [b]										
Model	R	R Square	Adjusted R Square	Std. Error of the Estimate	Change Statistics				Durbin-Watson
					R Square Change	F - Value	df1	df2	Sig. F Change	
1	.397a	0.158	0.149	11.97225	.158	19.230	6	617	.000	1.248
a. Predictors: (Constant), Job Enrichment Factor, Work Life Imbalance Factor, Job Structure Factor, Work Hindrance Factor, Job Enlargement Factor, Job Description Factor										
b. Dependent Variable: Quality Work Life										

Table 57 reveals that OLS Model has a goodness of fit for multiple regression analysis and the linear combination of Job Structure Factor, Work Hindrance Factor, Job Enlargement Factor and Job Enrichment Factor is significantly related to Quality of Work Life, { $F = 19.230$, $p<0.001$ }. The multiple correlations coefficient is 0.397, indicating that 15.8% of the variance of the respondent's quality of work life in the order of influence, is accounted by linear combination of Job Structure Factor, Work Hindrance Factor, Job Enlargement Factor and Job Enrichment Factor is significantly and positively influence quality of work life of the respondents. Whereas, Job Description Factor and Work Life Imbalance Factor do not have no significant influence on total quality of work life.

4.3 CONCLUSION:

This chapter shows hoe the data which were Collected is broken down with the help of statistical analysis for better understanding and validation. Statistical analysis is done using SPSS software package. Statistical analysis tools namely, Percentage Analysis, Factor Analysis, Descriptive Statistics, T-Test And F-Test, Cluster Analysis, Discriminant Analysis, Multiple Regression Analysis, Structural Equation Model (SEM) were used and understanding were interpreted. Based on the statistical analysis depicted in this chapter findings are summarized and showcased in the next chapter along with the relevant suggestions and conclusion .

Chapter V

SUMMARY OF FINDINGS, SUGGESTIONS AND CONCLUSION

CHAPTER – V

SUMMARY OF FINDINGS, SUGGESTIONS AND CONCLUSION

5.1 INTRODUCTION:

This chapter presents the summary of the preceding chapters, suggest measures for policy decision based on the inputs received during the fieldwork and also highlight the scope for future research.

5.2 MAJOR FINDINGS OF THE STUDY

The major findings of the study were explained in detailed manner. The results were presented in two sections with reference to women employees behavior towards the stress in the organisation..

DEMOGRAPHIC CHARACTERISTICS OF WOMEN EMPLOYEES

The responses of consumers are classified into three, namely demographic segmentation, employee characteristics and behavioural segmentation. The major findings were presented below.

The Demographic profile of the women employees consist of Age, Educational Qualification, Monthly Income, Area of Living, Nature of family and Marital Status. In addition the employee characteristics consist of Nature of Organisation, Schedule of Work, Level of employment, Experience (Years) and Working Hours per day in the organisation. In this study, the majority of respondents are married (64.9%), hailing from nuclear families (64.3%) and living in urban areas (55.3%) and earning monthly income between Rs.20,001 and Rs.40,000. Further, sizeable portion of the respondents are aged between 31 years and 40 years (41.0%) and post-graduates (39.7%). Furthermore the employees characteristics empirical result found that the majority of the respondents are working in private sector (82.4%) organisations, day shift (51.1%) work schedule and sizeable portion of the respondents are working in middle level (47.1%) designations. Further, descriptive statistics proves that average experience of the respondents is 7.90 years with the standard deviation value of 4.421 years and average working hours per day is 8.37 hours with the standard deviation value of 1.450.

DIMENSIONS INFLUENCING CAUSES OF STRESS AND QUALITY WORK LIFE

The exploratory factor analysis has been attempted to determine the dimensions to influencing the causes of stress and quality work life of the women employees. The extracted factor on each constructs is given below:

Organisational Causes of Stress: Two factors were identified and named as job description factor and job structure factor.

Personal Causes of Stress: Two factors were identified and named as work life imbalance factor and work hindrance factor.

Importance Reduce Stress: Two factors were found and named as job enlargement factor and job enrichment factor.

Quality of Work Life: Three factors were determined and it has been named as organisational culture factor, job precision factor and job ontogenesis factor.

Furthermore, the descriptive statistics and normality distribution statistics has been applied in order to determine the data distribution normally. The result proves that the empirical results of identified dimensions are normally distributed.

FORMATION OF CAUSES OF STRESS AND QUALITY WORK LIFE GROUPS

Cluster and Discriminant Analysis has been applied to identify the major groups of causes of stress and quality of work life among the women employees in the Chennai city.

Organisational Causes of Stress Groups: The women employees have been classified into three major OCS groups of the Highest Organisational Stress Group, Moderate Organisational Stress Group and Low Organisational Stress Group significantly differentiated by both the two Organisational Causes of Stress Factors along with two discriminant functions of Description and Structure.

Personal Causes of Stress Groups: The women employees have been classified into three major OCS groups of the High Personal Stress Group, Moderate Personal Stress Group and Low Personal Stress Group significantly differentiated by both the two Personal Causes of Stress Factors along with two discriminant functions of Imbalance and Hindrance.

Importance to Reduce Stress Groups: The women employees have been classified into three major IRS groups of the Highest Importance Group, Higher Importance Group and High Importance Group significantly differentiated by both the two Importance to Reduce Stress Factors along with two discriminant functions of Enlargement and Enrichment.

Quality Work Life Groups: The women employees have been classified into three major QWL groups of the Highest Work Life Group, Higher Work Life Group and High Work Life Group significantly differentiated by all the three Quality Work of Life Factors along with two discriminant functions of Culture and Ontogenesis.

MEAN DIFFERENCE BETWEEN DEMOGRAPHIC CHARACTERISTICS WITH RESPECT TO DIMENSIONS OF CAUSES STRESS TOTAL SCORE AND ITS FACTORS AND QUALITY WORK LIFE TOTAL SCORE AND ITS FACTORS

Significance of difference in personal characteristics and employment characteristics of the respondents with respect to organisational causes of stress total score and factors:

- The independent sample t-test results proves that there is a no mean significance difference between organisational causes of stress total score and its factors with respect to area of living among urban area and semi urban of the respondents.
- The independent sample t-test results proves that the respondents hailing from nuclear family group and joint family group have a significant mean difference with the organisational causes of stress total score and its factors such as job description and job structure of respondents.
- The independent sample t-test result proves that the respondents marital status, nature of organisation together have no significance mean difference between the dimension of the organizational cause of stress with respect to the Job description and job structure and total score of organisational causes of stress.
- The one way ANOVA results proves that the respondents age, educational qualification and income have no significance mean difference between the dimension of the organizational cause of stress with respect to the Job description and job structure and total score of organisational causes of stress.

- The one way ANOVA results proves that there is a significant difference between nature of the job shift working and dimensions of organisational causes of stress with respect to job description factor and job structure factor and total score of organisational causes of stress.
- The one way ANOVA results proves that the level of the employment of the respondents with respect to low level, middle level and higher level employment have a significant difference in the job description factor, job structure factor and total score of organisational causes of stress.

Significance of difference in personal characteristics and employment characteristics of the respondents with respect to personal causes of stress total score and factors:

- The independent sample t-test result proves that the respondents area of living, nature of the family, marital status, nature of organisation this all the demographic characteristics have no significance mean difference between the dimensions of personal causes of stress with respect to work life imbalance factor, work hindrance factor and total score of personal causes of stress.
- The one way ANOVA result proves that the respondents age and level of employment together have no significance mean difference between the dimensions of personal causes of stress with respect to work life imbalance factor, work hindrance factor and total score of personal causes of stress.
- The one way ANOVA result proves that the respondents educational qualification and income level have a significance difference between the dimensions of personal causes of stress with respect to work life imbalance factor and work hindrance factor and total score of personal causes of stress.

Furthermore, that the nature of the job of the respondents have a significant difference between the dimension of personal causes of stress with respect to the work hindrance factor.

Significance of difference in personal characteristics and employment characteristics of the respondents with respect to importance to reduce stress total score and factors

- The independent sample t-test result proves that the respondents area of living, nature of the family and marital status this demographic characteristics have no significance mean difference between the dimensions of importance to reduce stress with respect to job enlargement factor and work enrichment factor and total score of importance to reduce stress

- The independent sample t-test result proves that the nature of the organization working of the respondents private and public sector organisation have no significant difference between the dimensions of importance to reduce stress with respect to the job enlargement factor and total score of importance to reduce stress. Furthermore, there is no significant difference between the job enrichment factor with the importance to reduce stress

- The one way ANOVA result proves that the respondents age, educational qualification, income and level of employment this demographic characteristics together have no significance mean difference between the dimensions of importance to reduce stress with respect to job enlargement factor and work enrichment factor and total score of importance to reduce stress.

- The one way ANOVA result proves that the job nature of the respondents has significant difference between the dimensions of importance reduce stress with respect to job enlargement factor and the job enrichment factor and total score of the importance reduce stress.

Significance of difference in personal characteristics and employment characteristics of the respondents with respect quality of work life total score and factors

- The independent sample t-test result proves that the respondents area of living and marital status together have no significance mean difference between the dimension of quality of work life with respect to organizational culture factor, job precision and job ontogenesis and total score of the quality work life.
- The nature of family type of the respondents such as nuclear family and joint family groups have a significant mean difference between the dimensions of quality of work life with respect to organizational culture factor and job precision factor and total score of the quality of work life. Furthermore, there is no significant difference between the job ontogenesis factor.
- The nature of the organization such as private and public sector organisation respondents working has significant difference between the dimensions of quality work life with respect to organizational culture factor, job precision factor and job ontogenesis and total score of the quality work life.
- The One way ANOVA result proves that the age group of the respondents has significant difference between dimensions of quality work life with respect to organizational culture factor. Furthermore, the tables shows that there is no

significant difference between the job precision factor and job ontogenesis factor and total score of quality work life dimension.

- The educational qualification of the respondents has significant difference between the dimensions of quality work life with respect to job precision factor and job ontogenesis factor and total score of the quality work life. Furthermore, that there is no significant difference between the dimension of quality of work life with respect to organizational culture factor.

- The income level of the respondents has no significant difference between the dimensions of quality work life with respect to the organizational culture factor, job precision factor and job ontogenesis factor and total score of the quality work life.

- The nature of the job of the respondents shift wise working has significant difference between the dimensions of quality work life with respect to the organizational culture factor, job precision factor and job ontogenesis factor and total score of quality work life.

- The employment level of the respondents has significant difference between the dimensions of quality work life with respect to organizational culture and total score of quality work life. Furthermore, that there is no significant difference between the job precision factor and job ontogenesis factor.

STRUCTURAL EQUATION MODEL ON DETERMINANTS OF QUALITY OF WORK LIFE OF WOMEN EMPLOYEES

The structural equation model indicates that it has goodness-of-fit and it clearly explores that organisational causes of stress have significant and negative influence on quality of work life whereas, personal causes of stress and importance to reduce stress have significant and positive prediction for the inducement in the quality of work life of women employees. Except Job Description factor all the other stress factors have significant relationship with the quality of work life.

INFLUENCE OF STRESS ON QUALITY OF WORK LIFE OF WOMEN EMPLOYEES

The multiple regression analysis result explored that the respondent's quality of work life in the order of influence, is accounted by linear combination of Job Structure Factor, Work Hindrance Factor, Job Enlargement Factor and Job Enrichment Factor is significantly and positively influence quality of work life of the respondents.

5.3 SUGGESTIONS

- It is necessary to identify early warning signs in the body that tell when an individual is getting stressed such as feeling irritable, short tempered, losing track of time, clammy hands. As these signs vary from one person to another, the management of the concerned organization should take initiative to appoint a qualified person for identifying these warnings and removing them during the initial stage itself.
- It is suggested that the organization should encourage every women employees to prepare a to-do-list which should contain all anticipatable rhythms and routines like regular time for meal, sleeping, waking, exercise and relaxation, planning ahead for job. This will acts as an inducement to the women employees to remain organized which will help to curb the source of stress.

- It is found from the study that majority of the respondents are of the neutral opinion about the aim of the company training programme to improve their interpersonal skills among employees irrespective of the sector they are employed. Therefore company should take initiative to implement interactive training sessions to improve the communication among the employees which will pave for better interpersonal skills.
- Every women employee working in public sectors should be provided with personality development training course/ programme so that they become updated to match the skills needed in the career market.
- Job security being one of the main determinants of stress should be addressed by the company in a procedural way by making provisions for ensuring the security of the job so that this factor does not act as inducing factor for stress.
- The private organizations should take steps to provide customized career development training for their women employees to meet the global market requirement and equip themselves with an upgraded skill so that they are updated enough to sell their services in the career market.
- The company should arrange for special counselling session with every employees after their year reviews so that employees mental trauma are shared and get reduced after counselling sessions. This will also help to identify the individual specific training needs which will have a positive effective on the employees.
- It is important for both public and private sector to pay attention to their leave policy. Every women employee should be allowed to take

leave during their monthly menstrual period , as it is found that many women employees are under stress during their monthly menstruation and accordingly changes has to be made in the leave policy of the company

- Both the sectors should take effective initiative to arrange for proper rest rooms with adequate sanitary and water facilities for their women employees as it is found that majority of the concern is not providing clean and well maintained rest rooms which lowers the morale and acts as a source of dis-satisfaction.

- Sexual advances is still acting as a major source of stress. Many women employees are finding it difficult to work under certain supervision or boss because of such advances. Therefore it is necessary for the organization to establish sexual harassment cells which should properly look into grievances and take action on the guilty person.

- It is evident from the study the majority of the women employees are finding it difficult to have effective communication with their peers or supervisors due gender disparity. This hindrance has to be removed by the concerned management by instituting clear and transparent channel of communication. Any official failing to move through the prescribed channel of communication should be made answerable to the higher officials.

- There should be proper grievance handling procedure implemented. Disciplinary action should be taken on any person using filthy or abusive languages within the company. This will ensure the trust and security for the working womens.

- Stress always has a direct effect on the health of an individual. It is important for the management of the organization irrespective of the sector women employees are employed in to arrange for regular wellness programme and counselling sessions with qualified psychologists which help the women employees to limit the negative effects of their so that it does not have any negative influence on their quality of working life at the company.

- Domestic management programme can be organized to encourage spouses of women employees to take better charge of managing their homes and create a stress free and happy home environment.

- It is found that initial anxiety is one of the main source of stress and it can be removed if the company lends a helping hand to new joined employees by mentoring them. The new appointees are relieved from stress and this mentoring acts as a helping hand which they can hold till their anxiety reduces.

- Getting support from their supervisors or boss is also a major challenge for the women employees. In order to get support from supervisors, employers should initiate it in terms of leadership by example or self-commitment. They should provide proper tools and equipment; adequate training and other inputs needed by the people for successfully performing their jobs.

- One of the important motivational tool is empowerment which makes the women employees independent by giving them the means, ability and authority to do the work. Empowerment means giving people the power, authority, freedom and responsibility to carry out their jobs. It also gives them a sense of control over their work and makes them feel worthy of doing things on their own. Empowerment leads to greater job satisfaction and sense of control, which can result in better commitment and loyalty. For this purpose the employees should be given greater freedom to take part in the decision making process. This will make them not only empowered but also improves their trust towards the company

- Employees should be encouraged to practice self-management strategies. The management should take initiative to identify those employees with lower confidence, morale and with concentration problems. Those employees should be trained to use cognitive strategy which will help to build self-confident and optimism about doing a difficult task.

- The management should allocate fund for appointing qualified trainers to help the women employees to come out of their stress. The behavioural strategy for self-management such as self-reward, self- goal setting and other methods should be imparted to the women employees so that they can self-analyse their behaviour and reaction to different situations.

- It has been found that balancing their work life with personal life is a big issue for the women employees. The company should not take this issue lightly and should introduce work life balance initiative programmes like work from home and job sharing option to those women employees who have dependents care at home, flexi time to those women employees who face the difficulty of commutation.

- The management should follow equality in the pay scale. There should not be any differences in the salary paid to the employees working in the same grade/designation as it will lead to status issues within the organization and will affect the internal satisfaction of the employees.
- Proper transparent feedback mechanism should be instituted by the management. Every employee should be allowed to give feedback for the organizations initiatives and moves. This will help the management to identify the loopholes if any and should make necessary amendments in the same. The management should review their HR policy and should inculcate the above mentioned suggestions to continue the same in the long run.

5.4 CONCLUSION

Stress is inevitable in human life and it is the spice of life. It cannot be avoided and every individual employee irrespective of their job pressure will face stress. Complete freedom from stress comes only in death. The only thing that can be avoided is the negative consequences of stress. Stress can lead to both positive and negative consequences .However positive stress is necessary for an individual employee to work in the effective manner which will have a positive impact on his performance and will enhance the productivity of the organization as a whole. QWL is the need of the hour. Since quality of work life revolves around an individual personality, QWL can said to be directly impacted by the work stress of the individual employee. In order to retain the good talented employees within the organization and reduce the stress level ,it is important for the organization to have high quality of working life. Keeping in mind the role of QWL in reducing the stress level the current study is undertaken with a view to find out the impact of stress on the quality of working life of women employees. It has been found that different level of stress does impact the quality of working life of the women employees. Further it have been found that majority of the respondents are stressed out because of peer and supervisor pressure rather than job pressure. It is suggested that management should clearly dictate the roles and responsibilities of each employee and the time limit within which the given deadline should be completed should also be communicated so that they don't have to face unnecessary peer or supervisor pressure.

It is evident from the finding of the study that quality of work life is a critical concept that might be disturbed due to dissatisfaction of mind set. However if the companies focus on their employee's welfare by providing them a better and attractive compensation policy, optimum work load and by providing a superior work environment. In addition to the above said suggestions further it is said that the private companies should create a career growth opportunity within their environment that may lead to a better performance and therefore a better productivity. When there is a participatory management they will have an opportunity to participate with their ideas which will increase the enthusiasm of women employees . High degree of QWL leads to job satisfaction which ultimately results in effective and efficient performance. A happy employee will always have healthy mental health with low stress level and it will give better turnover, helps to make good decisions and finally positively contributes to organizational goal. An assured good quality of work life will not only attract young and new talents but will also help to retain the existing experienced talents which has become a big challenge in the current situation. The intrusion of personal life in work and work in personal life must also be balanced effectively so as to ensure that even when the women employees are running at their peak potential they are free from stress and strain. Since nowadays women employees are contributing more towards the socio- economic development of the country and their participation in the workforce has become necessary, every organization should take promotional measures and initiatives to attract more women employees and retain them in the long run. So it is up to the organization to focus on their women employees and improve their quality of work life so that attrition, absenteeism and decline in workers 'productivity can be checked.

5.5 SUGGESTION FOR FURTHER STUDIES:

The findings of the current study is limited in its scope with respect to various aspects. The results can be more elaborate and can help the society as whole to overcome the future problems when further research in the area is conducted. Hence the following area is suggested for further research in the future,

- A factor comparison of quality of work life of working women's in Chennai with respect to select variables can be made.

- The study can be made to find put which factors of quality of working life acting as source of stress among working women's.

- A comparative study on impact of stress on quality of working life between women working in private sector and public sector can also be undertaken in the future to get a better picture about the sector in which employees are having high stress level and to identify which sector has better quality of working life.

- The study can also be extended to identify the impact of stress on the job satisfaction among the women employees and the relationship of stress with the morale of the employees which will pave way for identifying the job satisfaction level.

- The researcher can undertake moderation effect on various sources of stress and quality of work life can be analyzed on the basis of various parameters like organizational culture, job satisfaction, morale etc., of working women's.

- Further the impact of occupational stress on the psychological contract of the women employees can also be studied.

- Since women's working in Chennai city is concentrated for the current study for the purpose of selecting representative sample the results can be validated by taking samples from other cities within Tamilnadu.

BIBLIOGRAPHY

BIBLIOGRAPHY

- Adelmann, P. K. (1987). Occupational complexity, control, and personal income: Their relation to psychological well-being in men and women. Journal of Applied Psychology, 72(4), 529-537. http://dx.doi.org/10.1037/0021-9010.72.4.529

- Ambrose Jones , III, , Cynthia P. Guthrie, , Venkataraman M. Iyer, (2012), Role Stress and Job Outcomes in Public Accounting: Have the Gender Experiences Converged?, in Donna Bobek Schmitt (ed.) Advances in Accounting Behavioral Research (Advances in Accounting Behavioral Research, Volume 15) Emerald Group Publishing Limited, pp.53 – 84

- Chet E. Barney, Steven M. Elias, (2010) "Flex-time as a moderator of the job stress-work motivation relationship: A three nation investigation", Personnel Review, Vol. 39 Issue: 4, pp.487-502, https://doi.org/10.1108/00483481011045434

- Christin Moeller, Greg A. Chung-Yan, (2013) "Effects of social support on professors' work stress", International Journal of Educational Management, Vol. 27 Issue: 3, pp.188-202, https://doi.org/10.1108/09513541311306431

- Darwish A. Yousef, (2002) "Job satisfaction as a mediator of the relationship between role stressors and organizational commitment: A study from an Arabic cultural perspective", Journal of Managerial Psychology, Vol. 17 Issue: 4, pp.250-266, https://doi.org/10.1108/02683940210428074

- Edna Rabenu, Aharon Tziner, Gil Sharoni, (2017) "The relationship between work-family conflict, stress, and work attitudes", International Journal of Manpower, Vol. 38 Issue: 8, pp.1143-1156, https://doi.org/10.1108/IJM-01-2014-0014

- Elizabeth George, Zakkariya K.A., (2015) "Job related stress and job satisfaction: a comparative study among bank employees", Journal of Management Development, Vol. 34 Issue: 3, pp.316-329, https://doi.org/10.1108/JMD-07-2013-0097

- Emma Donaldson-Feilder and Rachel Lewis (2011). Management competencies for preventing and reducing stress at work: identifying and developing the management behaviours Issued: July 2011 Registered charity no.1079797 doi: http://www.hse.gov.uk/research/rrhtm/rr633.htm

- Garima Mathur, Silky Vigg, Simranjeet Sandhar, Umesh Holani, (2007) "Stress as a correlate of job performance: a study of manufacturing organizations", Journal of Advances in Management Research, Vol. 4 Issue: 2, pp.79-85, https://doi.org/10.1108/97279810780001261

- Hamed Rashidian, Towhid Pourrostam 2016 Causes And Consequences Of Job Stress In Construction Projects International Journal Of Advances In Mechanical And Civil Engineering, Volume-3, Issue-2, Apr.-2016 ISSN: 2394-2827

- Hyo Sun Jung, Hye Hyun Yoon, (2016) "Why is employees' emotional intelligence important?: The effects of EI on stress-coping styles and job satisfaction in the hospitality industry", International Journal of Contemporary

Hospitality Management, Vol. 28 Issue: 8, pp.1649-1675, https://doi.org/10.1108/IJCHM-10-2014-0509

- Iram Batool Momina Abid Ruqia Safdar Bajwa (2016) Emotional Intelligence in Relation to Occupational Stress among Employees: A Study of Multan City IJournals: International Journal of Social Relevance & Concern Volume 4 Issue 6 JUNE 2016 ISSN-2347-9698

- Jennifer Walinga, Wendy Rowe, (2017) "Transforming stress in complex work environments: Exploring the capabilities of middle managers in the public sector", International Journal of Workplace Health Management, Vol. 6 Issue: 1, pp.66-88,

- Joyce E. Bono, Theresa M. Glomb, Winny Shen, Eugene Kim and Amanda J. KochBuilding (2016) A study on Effects Stress And Its Effects On Employees Productivity Published online before print September 6, 2016, doi:10.5465/amj.2011.0272ACAD MANAGE J December 1, 2016 vol. 56 no. 6 1601-1627

- Jacob Guinot, Ricardo Chiva, Vicente Roca-Puig, (2014) "Interpersonal trust, stress and satisfaction at work: an empirical study", Personnel Review, Vol. 43 Issue: 1, pp.96-115, https://doi.org/10.1108/PR-02-2012-0043

- Jm. Kotteeswari., & S. Tameem Sharief (2014) OB Stress And Its Impact On Employees' Performance A Study With Reference To Employees Working In Bpos International Journal Of Business And Administration Research Review,Issn No. 2347 – 856x.

- Latha Krishnan (2014) Factors Causing Stress among Working Women and Strategies to Cope up Journal of Business and Management (IOSR-JBM) e-ISSN: 2278-487X, p-ISSN: 2319-7668. Volume 16, Issue 5. Ver. V (May. 2014), PP 12-17

- Lawrence R. Murphy, Joseph J. Hurrell, Jr, (1987) "Stress Management in the Process of Occupational Stress Reduction", Journal of Managerial Psychology, Vol. 2 Issue: 1, pp.18-23, https://doi.org/10.1108/eb043387

- Lena Låstad, Tinne Vander Elst, Hans De Witte, (2016) "On the reciprocal relationship between individual job insecurity and job insecurity climate", Career Development International, Vol. 21 Issue: 3, pp.246-261, https://doi.org/10.1108/CDI-03-2015-0046

- Manjunatha M K., and Dr.T.P.Renukamurthy. (2017). "STRESS AMONG BANKING EMPLOYEE- A LITERATURE REVIEW." International Journal of Research - Granthaalayah, 5(1), 206-213. https://doi.org/10.5281/zenodo.263976.

- Mini Amit Arrawatia1, Deepanshi 2017 A Study Of Stress Management On Private Banks Employees And Impact Of Stress On Employee's Performance And Health. International Journal Of Science And Technology And Management , Vol.No.6,Issue No.07,July 2017,Issn (O)02394 – 1537,Issn (P) 2394 – 1529

- Michael Shane Wood, Dail Fields, (2007) "Exploring the impact of shared leadership on management team member job outcomes", Baltic Journal of Management, Vol. 2 Issue: 3, pp.251-272, https://doi.org/10.1108/17465260710817474

- Mirjam Haus, Christine Adler, Maria Hagl, Markos Maragkos, Stefan Duschek, (2016) "Stress and stress management in European crisis managers", International Journal of Emergency Services, Vol. 5 Issue: 1, pp.66-81, https://doi.org/10.1108/IJES-12-2015-0026

- Mohajan, H.K. (2012), The Occupational Stress and Risk of it among the Employees, International Journal of Mainstream Social Science, 2(2): 17–34..

- Nandhini, M. Usha, & P. Palanivelu (2016) Stress Management and Coping Strategies With Reference To Garment Employees in Coimbatore District International Journal of Emerging Research in Management &Technology ISSN: 2278-9359 (Volume-5, Issue-3)

- Nayanthara De Silva, Rasika Samanmali, Harsha Lal De Silva, (2017)"Managing occupational stress of professionals in large construction projects", Journal of Engineering, Design and Technology, Vol. 15 Issue: 4, pp.488-504, https://doi.org/10.1108/JEDT-09-2016-0066

- Nasreen Zehra Riffat Faizan 2017 The Impact of Occupational Stress on Employees at Project Based Organizations (PBOs) in Pakistan International Journal of Applied Business and Management Studies; Vol. 2, No.1; 2017 ISSN 2548-0448.

- Maria Vakola, Ioannis Nikolaou, (2005) "Attitudes towards organizational change: What is the role of employees' stress and commitment?", Employee Relations, Vol. 27 Issue: 2, pp.160-174, https://doi.org/10.1108/01425450510572685

- Orly Michael, Deborah Court, Pnina Petal, (2009) "Job stress and organizational commitment among mentoring coordinators", International Journal of Educational Management, Vol. 23 Issue: 3, pp.266-288, https://doi.org/10.1108/09513540910941766

- Prakash B. Kundaragi 2015 WORK STRESS OF EMPLOYEE Kousali Institute of Management Studies, Karnatak University, Dharwad Vol-1 Issue-3 2015 IJARIIE-ISSN(O)-2395-4396

- Pratibha Goyal, ZahidNadeem2004 Organisational role stress among women executives in the corporate sector in Punjab 34 (2), ,page(s):6674 Issuepublished: June1,2004 https://doi.org/10.1177/004908570403400205

- Priyanka Chaudhary, Radha Krishan Lodhwal, (2017) "An analytical study of organizational role stress (ORS) in employees of nationalized banks: A case of Allahabad Bank", Journal of Management Development, Vol. 36 Issue: 5, pp.671-680, https://doi.org/10.1108/JMD-09-2015-0137

- Paul Bowen, Peter Edwards, Helen Lingard Keith Cattell 2014 Occupational stress and job demand, control and support factors among construction project consultants International Journal of Project Management 32 (2014) 1273–1284

- Pei Chen, Paul Sparrow, Cary Cooper, (2016) "The relationship between person-organization fit and job satisfaction", Journal of Managerial Psychology, Vol. 31 Issue: 5, pp.946-959, https://doi.org/10.1108/JMP-08-2014-0236

- Radha Damle 2016 Employee Performance A Function Of Occupational Stress And Coping: A Study On Central Government Employees International Journal of Applied Business and Management Studies; Vol. 2, No.1; 2017 ISSN 2548-0448

- Ritsa Fotinatos-Ventouratos, Cary Cooper, (2005) "The role of gender and social class in work stress", Journal of Managerial Psychology, Vol. 20 Issue: 1, pp.14-23, https://doi.org/10.1108/02683940510571612

- Robert Conti, Jannis Angelis, Cary Cooper, Brian Faragher, Colin Gill, (2006) "The effects of lean production on worker job stress", International Journal of Operations & Production Management, Vol. 26 Issue: 9, pp.1013-1038, https://doi.org/10.1108/01443570610682616

- Sandra A. Lawrence, , Ashlea C. Troth, , Peter J. Jordan, , Amy L. Collins, (2011), A Review of Emotion Regulation and Development of a Framework for Emotion Regulation in the Workplace, in Pamela L. Perrewé, Daniel C. Ganster (ed.) The Role of Individual Differences in Occupational Stress and Well Being (Research in Occupational Stress and Well-being, Volume 9) Emerald Group Publishing Limited, pp.197 – 263

- Sari Mansour, Diane-Gabrielle Tremblay, (2016) "Workload, generic and work–family specific social supports and job stress: Mediating role of work–family and family–work conflict", International Journal of Contemporary Hospitality Management, Vol. 28 Issue: 8, pp.1778-1804, https://doi.org/10.1108/IJCHM-11-2014-0607

- Sathyanaraynan 2011 A STUDY ON STRESS MANAGEMENT IN IT INDUSTRY Journal of Management Research and Development (JMRD), ISSN 2248 – 937X (Print) ISSN 2248 –9390(Online), Volume 1, Number 1, January - April (2011)

- Shamil George Naoum, Carlos Herrero, Charles Egbu, Daniel Fong, (2018) "Integrated model for the stressors, stress, stress-coping behaviour of construction project managers in the UK", International Journal of Managing Projects in Business, Vol. 11 Issue: 3, pp.761-782, https://doi.org/10.1108/IJMPB-07-2017-0071

- Sheena Johnson, Cary Cooper, Sue Cartwright, Ian Donald, Paul Taylor, Clare Millet, (2005) "The experience of work-related stress across occupations", Journal of Managerial Psychology, Vol. 20 Issue: 2, pp.178-187, https://doi.org/10.1108/02683940510579803

- Slavyanska V, Dimitrova V, Stankova K 2017 Stress Management As A Factor Of Project Success . International Information Technologies And Management Doi: 10.1111/J.1744-6570.1978.Tb02118.X

- Sonja Treven, Vojko Potocan, (2005) "Training programmes for stress management in small businesses", Education + Training, Vol. 47 Issue: 8/9, pp.640-652, https://doi.org/10.1108/00400910510633170

- Smith, M. Bruyns, S. Evans, (2011) "A project manager's optimism and stress management and IT project success", International Journal of Managing Projects in Business, Vol. 4 Issue: 1, pp.10-27, https://doi.org/10.1108/17538371111096863

- Tulsee Giri Goswami, Richa Burman 2015 Impact of Work stress on Job satisfaction and Psychological wellbeing amongst Police Officers: Workplace Support as Moderator International Journal of Engineering Technology, Management and Applied Sciences September 2015, Volume 3, Special Issue, ISSN 2349-4476

- Vathsala Wickramasinghe, (2012) "Supervisor support as a moderator between work schedule flexibility and job stress: Some empirical evidence from Sri Lanka", International Journal of Workplace Health Management, Vol. 5 Issue: 1, pp.44-55, https://doi.org/10.1108/17538351211215384

- Xavior Selvakumar & S. Lawrence Immanuel (2015) - A Study on Stress Management of Employees at Commercial Banks with Special Reference to State Bank of India - Asia Pacific Journal of Research Vol. I. Issue XXVI.

- Yan-Hong Yao, Ying-Ying Fan, Yong-Xing Guo, Yuan Li, (2014) "Leadership, work stress and employee behavior", Chinese Management Studies, Vol. 8 Issue: 1, pp.109-126, https://doi.org/10.1108/CMS-04-2014-0089.

- Yitzhak Fried, Kendrith M. Rowland, Gerald R. Ferristhe 2006 Physiological Measurement of Work Stress: A Critique Doi: 10.1111/J.1744-6570.1984.Tb00528.X

CPSIA information can be obtained
at www.ICGtesting.com
Printed in the USA
BVHW091653131022
649382BV00015B/644

9 782300 875557